BADMINTON

BADMINTON

a celebration by

ANGELA RIPPON

Foreword by Virginia Leng

PAVILION
MICHAEL JOSEPH

First published in Great Britain in 1987 by
Pavilion Books Limited
196 Shaftesbury Avenue
London WC2H 8JL
in association with
Michael Joseph Limited
27 Wrights Lane, Kensington
London W8 5TZ

Designed by Lawrence Edwards
Co-ordinated by Susan Mitchell

British Library Cataloguing in Publication Data

Rippon, Angela
Badminton.
1. Badminton Horse Trials — History
I. Title
798.2'4   SF295.7

ISBN 1-85145-082-3

Printed and bound in Great Britain by
Hazell, Watson & Viney Ltd, Aylesbury, Bucks.

CONTENTS

Foreword   *Page 6*

Introduction   *Page 8*

Early Days   *Page 11*

The Sport Grows   *Page 20*

The Course   *Page 37*

The Director   *Page 56*

Money Matters   *Page 65*

As Seen on Television   *Page 74*

Behind the Scenes   *Page 87*

The Event   *Page 103*

The Winner   *Page 144*

Badminton Highlights   *Page 160*

Appendices   *Page 181*
List of Winners since 1949
Dressage
Speed and Endurance
Jumping

Index   *Page 188*

FOREWORD

The Badminton Horse Trials are to eventing what Wimbledon is to tennis or Wembley is to football. It is the ambition of every event rider to become good enough to compete at Badminton; the ultimate dream to be among the winners. It is not, though, only for competitors and others involved in the sport that Badminton is special. It also holds a unique place in the minds of the many thousands of enthusiastic followers of eventing. It is said to represent the greatest challenge to horses and to their riders, perhaps because they have to be able to perform well together in three rather different disciplines – dressage, cross-country riding and show jumping. The sport is therefore of interest to dressage riders, those whose preference is for hunting or other forms of crosscountry riding, and for those whose main interest lies in the showjumping ring. It also has tremendous appeal for people who like horses but do not themselves ride; it is, of course, partly thanks to television that three-day evening, which is an exciting spectator sport and one that comes across very well on the small screen, has become so popular. But hundreds of thousands of people prefer to go and see for themselves – so many, in fact, that it nowadays causes a major headache for the organizers of the competitions, as you will discover when you read the book.

If three-day events represent the ultimate equestrian sport, Badminton is the sport's ultimate challenge. It has become the most important horse trials, not only for the British but on the world eventing scene as well. It is the most demanding, most gruelling test. Every year the courses become harder, thanks to the devilish mind of Frank Weldon, whose course-building and organizational skills are largely responsible for the success of the event. At Badminton the test comes more in the demands made by the event itself, rather than in trying to beat the other competitors: the competition lies first and foremost between yourself and your horse, on the one hand, and what lies in store for you in the various phases of the competition, on the other. Is your horse calm and obedient enough to do his dressage test smoothly, and at the same time fit and bold enough to cope with the demands of roads and tracks, steeplechase and cross-country on the second day; if both of you survive that, will you have enough stamina not to disgrace yourselves in the show jumping ring in the final element of the contest? Winning at Badminton must, I suppose, be the ultimate goal, but it seems more important just to make it to the end of the competition – enough of a challenge in itself, particularly when you are walking the cross-country course before the event begins, and new, ever more daunting fences loom at you.

I have competed at Badminton for a number of years, and have discovered that you can never be complacent about it. The thrill of being there, the butterflies, the friendliness and support of those around you, the sensation of adrenalin pumping violently round your system as you wait your turn to go – none of that changes, no matter how experienced a rider you are, how successful you have been in the past. I have a special affection for Badminton because I live so close by, and enjoy so much support from local people when I am competing. But I know that for everyone involved, for those behind the scenes on the organizational side, for competitors, grooms and other helpers, and even for the television crews, it is a unique event. The time I was first presented with the little silver horse that is awarded to the top twelve riders was one of the best moments of my life – almost as good as actually winning!

Angela Rippon brings three valuable skills to her story about Badminton. She is a horsewoman herself, and is therefore able to appreciate what is involved for the horses and the riders who compete. She is a very experienced interviewer, so the time she spent talking to everyone connected with the event elicited a great deal of inside information that makes engrossing reading. Her journalistic skills, both on radio and television and through the written word, enable her really to bring alive the atmosphere and excitement – the tragedy and hilarity, the hard work and the dedication, the triumphs and disasters, the agony and the ecstasy of the event. These feelings are also captured in the numerous illustrations that themselves really do show what it is like to be there.

Anyone interested in eventing in general, as well as Badminton in particular, could not fail to find this book fascinating. I certainly have.

Virginia Leng 1986

INTRODUCTION

I can pin point exactly the first time I was ever aware of Badminton. It was in 1972. I'd only been riding a year or so myself. I was a very keen, but unaccomplished newcomer to the pleasures of week-end hacking. One of my horse-mad girlfriends broached the idea of going to Badminton to see the three-day event. We might as well have been going to Japan to watch Sumo wrestling for all I knew – but we went, and I was hooked.

On the Friday, I sat in the stands, and watched with genuine admiration and pleasure as a procession of riders and their horses performed with apparent ease and fluidity a sequence of controlled movements, the key to which was still a complete mystery to me. On Saturday I gaped open-mouthed at the solid timber and startling proportions of the cross country fences, and got withering looks from officionadoes every time I gasped, or shrieked loudly whenever a horse and rider powered over the obstacles. As a complete green horn I was convinced that they would all collide with the timbers and come crashing down in a muddle of broken or bruised limbs. While it's all very well for the initiated to scoff and say 'don't be so daft', believe me, for anyone with a non-horsy background, being confronted for the first time with the guts and power of the competitors doing battle over three foot eleven of Frank Weldons timber is an awesome experience.

And then to round off that first Badminton experience there was the sight on Sunday afternoon of Richard Meade making an oh so careful round in the show jumping ring, and just losing the championship in the final seconds to Lt. Mark Phillips and his horse Great Ovation. What a tremendous first Badminton that was for me. Subsequently I went year after year, with friends and family to watch Eventing at its very best, and hope that my own less ambitious efforts in the saddle would benefit from just a few hours of being in the same arena as some of the finest riders in the world. A sentiment which I suspect would be echoed by several thousand of those who make the trip to Badminton every Spring.

In 1981 I had the rare and privileged experience of being able to observe Badminton from a competitor's point of view, without ever having to actually tackle the fences myself. In that year I wrote Captain (as he'd then become) Mark Phillips's biography and was able to watch and record his emotions and preparations for the championships for four months.

As a result of that experience, my respect and admiration for the riders and their horses was increased ten fold. Their courage, skill and determination puts them in a class of their own. While the Whitbread Championship quite clearly emerged as the classic annual three-day event in the world.

Although my own riding ambitions have more recently taken me into novice one-day events, I have no burning desire to tackle Badminton. Perhaps on the right horse on the right day I might be tempted to leap over the Whitbread Barrels, or even the Lamb Creep, but you wouldn't get me near the Normandy Bank, Horsen's Bridge, or the mighty leap over the corner at the Vicarage Vee for a king's ransom. Make no mistake about it, Badminton is not a competition for the faint hearted, or those merely 'flirting' with the sport. It's a testing ground for champions, where only the bravest and the best survive.

Certainly, one of the greatest pleasures for me, in researching this book, has been to meet many of the Equestrian 'greats': men and women whose names and reputations are woven inextricably into the fabric of Badminton. These are the competitors, the officials and 'characters' who've helped to write a bit of sporting history that is quintisentially British.

It has also been a pleasure to watch the Badminton 'machine' in operation. It runs smoothly in second gear for most of the year as fences are designed and built, and administrative details handled with deft professionalism. Then there is a smooth change through the gears as the band-wagon gains momentum and powers down the home straight to a successful conclusion with yet another worthy name added to the list of Badminton champions. It was a fascinating year's work, reading through old manuscripts, delving back into the early record books, and re-living through so many of the competitors the highlights of Badmintons past from 1949.

Badminton is a unique experience, for the competitors who annually accept its challenge, and for the spectators who flock to this corner of Gloucestershire to absorb the atmosphere and competition of the greatest equestrian championship in the world. As an author, and a Badminton enthusiast, I hope I've been able to capture at least some of that character through the pages of this book.

Angela Rippon 1986

1

EARLY DAYS

Imagine the scene. It is 12 August 1948, a warm sunny day, and the Duke and Duchess of Beaufort are enjoying a picnic lunch out of the back of their Land Rover on the hills overlooking the Royal Military College at Sandhurst. The Duke, whose religion was hunting and creed the superiority of British horseflesh and horsemanship over the rest of the world, had just watched the cross-country phase of the very first three-day event he had ever seen, in the equestrian division of the 1948 Olympic Games. The result must have made a huge dent in his patriotic pride. The British team – Major Peter Borwick on Liberty, Brigadier Lyndon Bolton on Sylveste and Major D. Stewart riding Dark Seal – was eliminated after Sylveste had two falls on the cross-country, and Dark Seal retired lame.

But in spite of the result – or maybe because of it – the Duke had been fascinated by the concept of a competition that demanded the qualities of skill and precision for dressage and show jumping, coupled with the flair and courage needed to ride over solid, fixed obstacles on a cross-country course. As he was often heard to remark in subsequent years, 'With our hunting background, this is a sport at which Britain should excel'. Clearly, what was needed was a competition run on the lines of an Olympic three-day event to give British horsemen the opportunity of practising and perfecting the relevant skills if they were to have any hope at all of breaking the dominance, in what was essentially a military sport, of Europe's cavalry officers. The Duke did not like losing, and was determined that by the 1952 Olympics Britain would field a winning team of three riders and horses. His own country seat, at Badminton in Gloucestershire, seemed to him to offer the ideal location, with a ready made point-to-point course, acres of land for the roads and

Colonel Trevor Horn, the first Director of the Badminton Horse Trials, with Prince Bernhard of The Netherlands.

tracks, and the rolling parkland around Badminton House the perfect arena for the cross-country phase.

He approached the British Horse Society, who thought it was an excellent idea, and agreed to give financial backing to the project. The first stage was to appoint a committee. The Duke, Vice Patron and Vice President of the Fédération Equestre Internationale (FEI), was invited to be President of the Badminton Committee. He was supported by Col. The Hon. C. 'Guy' Cubitt, at that time Chairman of the British Horse Society (BHS); Brigadier 'Bogey' Bowden-Smith, who had ridden in the 1924 Olympics, trained Britain's 1948 squad, and built the Aldershot Olympic course; Major Peter Borwick, who had ridden at Aldershot in the 1948 Games; Mr C. Cornell, in charge of finance; Lt.-Col. R. 'Babe' Moseley, a keen equestrian sportsman; and Col. Trevor Horn, who was appointed the first director and course builder. Trevor Horn would be the first to admit that his knowledge of the three-day event was 'decidedly limited'. As a council member of the BHS and former cavalry officer he had been seconded to help with the dressage competitions in the 1948 Olympics, but until the competition began had never seen a three-day event in his life.

The three-day event was originally a military competition conceived as a test of army chargers, and was called 'the Military'. The perfect cavalry horse was expected to be calm and obedient on parade, be agile and supple, responding to the lightest command from its rider during battle, have the stamina to survive a route march, jump any obstacle, be bold and fast over any terrain when carrying urgent messages in battle, and be fit enough to carry on day after day. All of those requirements were distilled down to a sort of equestrian triathlon of dressage on day one, show jumping on day three, with the gruelling speed and endurance phase sandwiched in between.

It was at the 1912 Olympics in Stockholm that equestrian sports first appeared, thanks to the efforts of Count Clarence von Rosen of Sweden – a country that excelled at the sport between the wars. Seven nations, including Britain, entered teams in the Military on that occasion, but no British rider completed the course. In 1924 Captain D. de Fonblanque came sixth in the individual placings at the Paris Olympics, while at the 1936 Berlin Olympics three officers trained at the British Cavalry School at Weedon in Buckinghamshire won the team bronze medal in the event.

By 1948 the Military or Olympic three-day event was still dominated by the Army, so when the Olympics came to London both the event, and the Grand Prix dressage were staged within the military training facilities of Aldershot. Col. Trevor Horn's duties were mainly confined to the dressage competition, as arena manager for both the Grand Prix dressage and the dressage section of the three-day event. As he later wrote in his journal, 'My duties were to see that the arena was correctly marked out and kept in a fit state and that the officials, judges and competitors were all there at the times stated. On the cross-country day I was to assist where necessary.' The 'assistance' amounted to accompanying the Duke on his walk round the cross-country course on that fateful day in August, and watching the seed of enthusiasm take root as they walked from fence to fence.

Within weeks of the 1948 Olympics passing into the history and the record books, the Badminton three-day event was born. Trevor Horn was about to start laying the foundations of what was to become one of Britain's major sporting

Above: Setting up one of the jumps at Badminton, April 1949, in the first year of the competition.
Right: One of the judges measures a jump at Badminton Great Park, April 1949.

events, the world's greatest annual three-day event, though he could have had no way of knowing that at the time. It was a daunting task. Not only was his knowledge of the event somewhat sparse, but considering that he was starting from scratch he did not have a great deal of time to stage the competition. While the Duke's great patriotism and enthusiasm prompted him to offer the Park and grounds for the competition, it did not run to interfering with his first and greatest passion – hunting. The event had to be staged out of the hunting season, and at a time when competitors and spectators would not interfere with the running of the Badminton estate and farm. April seemed to be the most convenient time, and so the date was set. The Badminton three-day event would begin on Wednesday 20 April with dressage, continue on Thursday with the speed and endurance and cross-country test, and finish on Friday 22 April with the show jumping. The BHS in London organized the advertising, the finance and schedules, then processed the entries. Trevor Horn began driving, riding and cycling around the Duke's estate at Badminton, measuring distances, getting to know every nook and cranny of the Park, and beginning to plan in his mind's eye the location and shape of the twenty-one fences on the first cross-country course.

The top of Trevor Horn's grand piano in the lounge of his home in the neighbouring village of Luckington became the Badminton office, while the front lawn was littered with poles as he worked out the size and construction of the individual obstacles. Badminton estate workers were roped in to help, sawing timber from the Duke's own woodland under the expert eye of head forester Charlie Chapple, and building the fences to Trevor Horn's instructions. The Duke's gardeners prepared the lawn directly in front of the house for the dressage arena, and Col. Horn raided the famous Blue Book – the official membership list of the

*Left: April 1949. Lt.-Col. C. P. D. Legard's horse Varne
slips on the shelving approaching the water jump.
Horse and rider were reunited uninjured and able to
complete the course.
Above: The dressage in progress in 1949 in front of
Badminton House.*

Beaufort Hunt – for the names of potential volunteers to act as stewards, judges
and general helpers throughout the three days, establishing a tradition that still
exists. Although the director had checked the length of each phase in the speed
and endurance section with a cyclometer attached to a bicycle, he wanted to make
sure that the horses would be able to complete the three miles of the cross-country
section within the maximum time allowed. The only way to check would be to get a
rider to go round the course, but as no competitor was allowed near the obstacles
until the competition itself Trevor Horn asked Lesley Rooke, daughter of the
commissioner to the Badminton estate, Major Nelson Rooke (and now Mrs John
Wooldridge), to time the course for him. Riding her own hunter she jumped over
those fences that were fairly straightforward and at the more daunting elements
rode up to the takeoff point, trotted round to the landing site while the stop
watches were reset, and then galloped off to the next obstacle. Her time was close
enough to the eleven minutes for the director to heave a sigh of relief. A few days
before the event, estate workers placed straw bales around the dressage arena to
provide temporary seating, and marked out a small car park immediately behind so
that enthusiasts could sit in or on their cars for a 'grandstand' view. There were
about half a dozen trade stands, but nothing so sophisticated as a public toilet!
Although the BHS had advertised the occasion, with an unwitting sense of destiny,

as 'the most important horse event in Great Britain', the truth was that they had no idea of just how many people would turn up – if any! Badminton, to most people in Britain, meant an indoor game played with shuttlecocks over a net. Even among the horsy set there was some confusion over what the whole thing was about. Dressage was not only alien to most riders in Britain at that time, it was generally viewed with considerable cynicism and distrust as being something performed by a 'load of pansies' in Europe, and although show jumping was gaining in popularity it was still a 'minority' sport. Only the cross-country phase struck a chord with the hunting and racing fraternity, who recognized the thrill and skill of galloping over natural obstacles. So then, as now, it was the cross-country day that attracted the majority of spectators: the 'county set' from Gloucestershire and the surrounding counties turned out in force – all one thousand or so of them.

If the spectators, and to some degree the competitors, were slightly dubious about this new competition, the Duke and his committee harboured no such doubts. The programme for that first year states categorically: 'The sole object of this annual competition, which will be held on His Grace's land at Badminton in 1949, 1950 and 1951, is to find riders and horses suitable for training as a team to compete at the Olympic Games in Helsinki in 1952.' So the event would run for three, possibly four years. The goal was an Olympic success. What happened after that was anybody's guess.

There were forty-seven horses and riders entered for the 1949 competition, of whom twenty-two actually ran, including the expected smattering of military men, several lady riders, and the Earl of Westmorland. For most riders it was all a bit of a lark, a great way to round off the hunting season. Nevertheless a few came with serious intent, including Captain Tony Collings, owner of the Porlock School of Equitation in North Devon and the man who was subsequently to mastermind Britain's assault on the eventing scene, and John Shedden from the Cotswold Equitation School – two men who rated among the finest horsemen in Britain, and though as 'professionals' they could never represent Britain in the Olympics, both were determined to make their mark at Badminton.

The competitors arrived throughout the Monday and Tuesday of competition week. Horses were stabled, then as now, in the magnificent stable block behind Badminton House (as all the Duke's hunters had been put out to grass for the summer!). Competitors were briefed in the main street of Badminton village, given a map showing the route for speed and endurance day, and then escorted round the course. They were told they could make a further inspection of the course, on foot, in their own time – but only after asking the permission of the director!

The dressage test was not taken too seriously by a number of competitors who came straight to the competition from the hunting field. Most scores were in the mid to upper hundreds, while W. Stokes on Dandy Dick clocked up a cricket score of 233, and still managed to finish thirteenth overall after the three days with a total score of 578! The efforts of those who had prepared for the event by paying extra attention to their dressage and show jumping were reflected in the leading scores. Tony Collings on Remus went into the lead with 56 points, while John Shedden and the five-year-old Golden Willow were third with 90. As an indication of how unsure the organizers were of the standards to be set in each phase, the dressage test of 1949 looked more like a test for a Grand Prix horse than an eventer. There were twenty movements that included two flying changes, a pirouette and two five-loop

Above: John Shedden on Golden Willow in 1949.
Right: The Hon. Guy Cubit at Badminton in 1948.

serpentines in counter canter. Marks were awarded out of ten for each movement, and multiplied by a coefficient that ranged from 5 to 30. The present FEI test is not anything like so demanding, with no flying changes and calling for only a three-loop serpentine. So perhaps it is no wonder that the dressage marks were so high!

On cross-country day competitors were set off at five-minute intervals, starting at two o'clock. Ahead of them nine miles of roads and tracks, two miles of steeplechase course and three miles on the cross-country phase. In addition to their map and the rather limited access to the course, the riders were assured that they would have no difficulty in following the course, which was well marked with flags, bunting and 'bits of paper'! The course began with Phase A at Hinnegar Lodge and went north towards Didmarton village, where competitors rode the steeple-chase course over the nine fences of the Didmarton point-to-point course. The second stage of roads and tracks dropped south, back into the Park at Worcester lodge, circled down through Bodkin Wood and back into the stable yard behind Badminton House via Little Badminton and the Keeper's Lodge. Phase D, the twenty-one fences of the cross-country course, started just behind the stable block and circled left handed towards Cape Farm beyond the Fatting Barn, over Luckington Lane and back towards Worcester Avenue via Allen Grove and the Hermit's Cell. Once over the last fence, riders had to complete a twelve hundred yard 'run in'. The fourteen miles was a continuous circuit – where one phase ended another began, with no compulsory halt before the cross-country section. Each phase had an optimum time; anyone taking less than the time allowed gained bonus points, those who went over the time collected penalty points – any competitor wanting to take a breather before riding either the steeplechase or the cross-country phases had to make sure he got to the finish of the previous section with minutes in hand.

Eight of the twenty-two starters were eliminated on the course, but John Shedden had the ride of his life on Golden Willow. He was a quality horse who ate up the roads and tracks at a steady hand canter, which took nothing out of him and left Shedden with eight minutes to spare before setting off over the big fences. Although Trevor Horn had never ridden in a three-day event, he was a hunting man who appreciated the value of big, bold fences that invited riders to jump with a fast, on-going stride. He described them as 'rigid' and, as far as possible, resembling natural objects: hedges, ditches, farm gates, brooks, streams, road crossings, barriers, etc. None was above the maximum height that still applies, 3ft 11 in. John Shedden especially remembers a huge parallel bars and 'formidable drop fence'. As the course was not roped, as it is now, competitors could take their own line to obstacles, knocking off vital seconds with short cuts. As Shedden says, 'The whole of Gloucestershire turned out for the day – but that wasn't many people, and if they got in the way, they soon moved when you shouted. They were horsy people, you see, and understood about that sort of thing.'

Cross-country day was wet and windy, but there was a holiday atmosphere about the place. To most spectators this was just a fancy point-to-point, and their informality affected the competitors. For all that he wanted to win the first Badminton, John Shedden even admits that 'going over the Luckington Lane I saw my sister in the crowd. I waved – so she and the rest of the crowd clapped and cheered, and we just kept going like a dose of salts.' Willow was not the easiest

Colonel Scott on Lady Diana comes to grief at one of the fences at Badminton in 1952. Rider and horse went on to finish the course.

horse to ride; he was inclined to take a hold, and in the following year dumbfounded the crowds when he jumped the Irish Bank in one leap. As John Shedden recalls: 'I would see one ear go forward, and one go back. That was the signal that told me, "Look out Shedden, we're in for a bumpy ride" and he'd just jump anything in sight.' Not surprisingly, Willow clocked up the fastest time of the day, gaining 63 bonus points, and shot into the lead, where he stayed in spite of ten penalties the following day for a fence down in the show-jumping ring.

Immediately after the three-day event jumping there were two competitions organized by the British Show Jumping Association (BSJA). Competitors included the young Pat Smythe, Ted Edgar, Mr W. C. Biddlecombe, and Andrew Massarella, whose cousin Ronnie Massarella is now chef d'équipe of the British show jumping team. They were all the brightest young stars of a sport growing in public appeal. The BHS knew that the extra competition would bring in the crowds and help to make the event a financial success in case the three-day event was not a sufficient attraction. In fact the event turned out to be a huge success with spectators and competitors alike, and they did make a small profit – certainly enough to cover the £400 in prize money offered to the 'eventers' (though the word had not been coined by then). The first prize of £150 went to the owner of the winning horse, Mrs Home Kidston. John Shedden, as the rider, received nothing, not even a rosette. But what he does have is the vivid memory of finishing on cross-country day feeling 'as you would at the end of a great day's hunting – absolutely marvellous' and the knowledge that his is the first name on a roll of honour that now includes European, World and Olympic champions, all winners of an event that has grown to be not just 'the most important horse event in Great Britain' but the greatest three-day event in the world.

2

THE SPORT GROWS

The 1952 Olympics were to be held in Helsinki, and while British field and track athletes had numerous athletic meetings around the country on which to hone their skills, and even the show jumpers could refine their performance at competitions being sponsored by the flourishing BSJA, the 'eventers' still had only Badminton as a once a year training ground for their unique sport. True, there were hunter trials being run around the country, usually by local hunt committees, show jumping competitions, and a growing number of people who could train riders and horses to the demanding disciplines of dressage. But no individual event brought all three elements together, over three days of competition. Badminton was the only showcase for riders and horses to demonstrate their ability, and from which Olympic selectors could make preliminary judgements on a possible team.

As the sport was so young no one assumed that the perfect combination of horse and rider would automatically merge as a ready made team. What the selectors were looking for was a promising horse, with a willing owner prepared to 'lend' it for a talented rider to partner.

The 1949 competition had been very much a case of testing the water, but by the end of the 1950 competition it was clear that Badminton was producing a few exciting possibilities. Tony Collings won on Remus. As a professional riding instructor he could not himself ride in the Games, but he was earmarked as an Olympic team trainer, while Remus was a definite possibility for the shortlist. The first winner, John Shedden, became the first man to ride two horses around the course by taking both Golden Willow and Kingpin. He was beaten into second place by just 2.75 points on Kingpin, and came fifth on Golden Willow after some dubious timekeeping on the cross-country course robbed him of valuable bonus points. Sadly, as John was also a professional and the horse belonged to an American, the partnership could not be considered.

Nor could any of the lady riders, who had done particularly well, as at that time equestrian women weren't allowed to represent their country in the Olympics.

Captain Tony Collings, winner in 1952 on Remus, in the show jumping ring.

However, on the plus side there was Reg Hindley and his own horse Stealaway, who had been placed eleventh the first year, and then sixth, at Badminton; and also a horse called Stella owned by Major John Miller (now Sir John Miller, the Queen's equerry). They had all demonstrated the sort of star quality the selectors were looking for. So, with two years still to go Badminton had highlighted at least one trainer, one rider and three horses showing Olympic potential. This was a beggarly store compared with today's riches, but considering that until then Olympic horsemen had been recruited solely from the cavalry school at Weedon by an Army instructor on the principle that 'you, you and you will compete in the three-day event', it was a veritable cornucopia.

There was still a long way to go, of course. Ideally, the selectors wanted sixteen horses to go into initial training, to be whittled down to ten by the April of 1952, from which the final three would be chosen, with six riders in contention for the three places in the team. In the early 1950s ideas about training and preparation were quite different from those held now, more than thirty years later, when people would expect to work for years on a horse and rider to produce a winning combination. In 1950 the selectors felt they still had at least a year's breathing space to find likely contenders, and no one found that time span unduly worrying.

If Badminton was seen by a growing number of enthusiasts as the main British testing ground for the Olympics, it did not take long for hunt committees in other parts of the country to latch on to the idea of running similar, though less ambitious, competitions to prepare riders and horses for Badminton itself. There were still some riders competing who had their sights set firmly on a place in the Olympic team, and others who regarded it as a great lark. Somewhere in the middle lay a growing number of competitors who saw Badminton as an end in itself – a championship to be won for its own prestige. And so, in 1951 the first one-day events began to appear. Gisbourne Park at Clitheroe in Lancashire was one of the first off the mark, while the Newmarket and Thurlow Hunt had a competition at Denston Hall on Thursday 5 April 1951 – just two weeks before that year's Badminton.

It described itself in the schedule as a 'test, run on similar lines to the BHS's Olympic Horse Trial – the Badminton Three-Day event – but is in a much simplified form', and went on to explain that 'the object of the test is to give riders an opportunity to practise, in public, over an easier and shorter course, and to encourage newcomers to try their hand at a comprehensive riding competition, where the good training of a horse and his ability to cross country are equally important.' The idea of a one-day event spread quickly, and within three years there were a dozen competitions all providing valuable training grounds for riders and horses who wanted to tackle the Olympic-sized challenge of the Badminton course.

Meanwhile Badminton itself went from strength to strength, in 1950 the *Daily Telegraph* gave a cup for the winning horse and owner, and the following year, in 1951, the competition declared itself to be 'open to the world', offering the first team championship of Europe. It changed its name to the 'Olympic Horse Trials at Badminton'. As a result there were competitors from Switzerland, Ireland and Holland to add to the increased British entry, but as only two Dutch riders appeared, and not the statutory three required for a team, the team competition was cancelled and riders had to compete as individuals. The weather that year was particularly vicious. It rained so hard that the cross-country course was flooded, and several jumps had to be resited and rebuilt before the competitors' briefing. Then a further flood of rain meant that even the second course could not be used, so a third course had to be prepared, which was not finished until late into the evening on dressage day.

At the end of day one, six Swiss and two Dutch riders held the top eight positions. Reg Hindley on Stealaway was the first British rider to show, at ninth, almost 70 points behind the leader, the Swiss rider Captain A. Blaser on Mahmud with 48.75. This was a clear indication of European superiority in a phase that many British riders had still not come to terms with.

The European horses were not particularly fit. The long, hard winter made it virtually impossible for them to train out of doors and improve stamina in time for an April competition, which is why so few Europeans still come to Badminton. But they were supple and obedient from months of work indoors, so while not

Dot Love riding The Professional at The Lake.

particularly fast over the cross-country course they made light work of the more complicated fences, like the Coffin, which needed to be ridden with careful precision. British riders and horses, on the other hand, used to the 'on-going' pace of the hunting field, found that fence, in particular, quite literally the graveyard of British aspirations, as horse after horse refused, fell or was eliminated.

National pride was salvaged by the young Jane Drummond-Hay, just out of Pony Club competitions, riding Happy Knight, who went fast and clear to finish the three days in second place. But it was Swiss cavalry officer Captain Hans Schwarzenbach on Vae Victis who won, with Swiss and Dutch riders taking seven of the top ten placings. But the result was not totally negative for Britain. Reg Hindley and Stealaway were again well placed at thirteenth, Major John Miller and Stella finished seventh, and a new horse, Starlight, made an impressive debut, finishing in eleventh place. Captain Michael Naylor-Leyland (finishing fifth on Torloisk) and Major Laurence Rook (fourteenth on Gold Pot) were two of the riders who made a good impression and were earmarked as possible Olympic contenders.

In October 1951 the selection committee had to settle on the horses and riders that would be sent to Tony Collings' training establishment at Porlock in North Devon to undergo six months of intensive training. The idea was that horses and riders would compete at the following year's Badminton, and after that the selectors would choose the combinations of three horses and riders to represent Britain in Helsinki.

For all that Badminton had proved itself to be a valuable testing ground for horses and riders, the truth was that by 1951 it really had not thrown up anything like enough contenders. True, there was Remus, who had won in 1950; Stealaway, who had competed three times finishing eleventh, sixth and thirteenth; Stella, who had been fifteenth in 1950 and seventh in 1951; and Starlight, who had finished eleventh at his first three-day event. But four horses that had proved themselves over the Badminton course were not enough. The selectors had to look beyond Badminton, to the winners from the many one-day events around the country, to make up their quota. So they included Bambi V, a six-year-old bay mare (who went on to win Badminton ridden by her owner, Margaret Hough, in 1954); Banbridge Boy, a 16 hand chestnut gelding owned by the Royal Marines; Philippa, an eleven-year-old brown mare; Savoyarde, an eight-year-old chestnut mare; and Speculation, an eight-year-old grey gelding out of Reg Hindley's stable. All of them had either won or come second at one-day events over the past two years. To them they added the Grade A show jumper Crispin, and Tudor Gal, a six-year-old brown mare who had won several point-to-points.

Those, then, were the four-legged Olympic hopefuls. As for the riders, they were an elite half dozen made up of Reg Hindley, who had won his spurs at Badminton, John Miller, Michael Naylor-Leyland and Laurence Rook, who had also had great success competing with the Army in Germany. Lieut. Cdr. John Oram was the only naval man in the squad, having notched up three consecutive seconds in one-day events on his own mare Philippa, while the sixth member of the team was Bertie Hill, a young farmer from North Devon who had never ridden in a one- or three-day event at all. Bertie Hill's inclusion in the team was entirely due to Tony Collings, who knew him to be a fine point-to-point and steeplechase jockey. Collings always maintained that if he could get three horses and riders to go clear and fast over the cross-country course, we would be in with a chance for a medal. Hill's speed and skill over the racing fences made him a natural as far as Collings was concerned, and in fact to this day Bertie Hill is regarded as the finest natural horseman Britain has ever produced.

Eleven horses and six riders were installed at Porlock, and began an intensive six months' training, with the Olympic gold medal their goal. Every day the riders did an hour, and eventually two hours of dressage with Herr Richard Waetjen – a baptism of fire for young Hill, who had barely heard of dressage, let alone done it! They all competed in as many local shows as possible to gain experience and to build stamina, with an outing to the one-day event at Stowell Park the final pipe opener before Badminton in April 1952.

The Olympic horses were all entered to run *hors concours*, riding only those parts of the event that the trainer and selection committee thought necessary. With the Olympics only three months away in July, they did not want to run the risk of injury limiting their choice. ·

Major (now Colonel) J. Miller and Stella at full stretch over the water jump in 1952.

J. R. Hindley on Speculation at the water jump in 1952.

Throughout the six months at Porlock, Tony Collings had insisted on each rider working with every one of the 'Olympic' horses, as well as every other horse he had in his yard. As Bertie Hill recalls, 'He had the perfect eye for pairing a particular rider with a particular horse. Everyone always thinks they can ride their horse better than anyone else. But that's not necessarily so. Very often you change the rider, and you'll make the thing tick.' And he goes some way towards explaining how it was that the selectors persuaded so many owners to allow their horses to go into training. 'With Tony it was always owners first,' he says. 'Riders knew that they were the lucky ones to be put up. It was the owners who were special, and because of that attitude, he could get any horse he wanted.'

At least three of the pairings for that Badminton were predictable. John Miller rode his own Stella, John Oram took Philippa and Bambi, while Reg Hindley rode his own Speculation. But Stealaway, who had been so successful for Reg Hindley at Badminton, was given to Bertie Hill to ride, along with Banbridge Boy, while Michael Naylor-Leyland was assigned Crispin. Laurence Rook had been mounted on Starlight, at the start of what was to be a highly successful partnership, but they were withdrawn before the competition along with Tudor Gal, Remus and Savoyarde, and would have to wait another year before conquering Badminton.

With seven of the country's top horses riding *hors concours*, the competiton that year was wide open. There were eight new fences on the course, including the Quarry, though it was that old bogey the Coffin that once again caused most grief on the second day. The weather was warm and sunny, it was an Olympic year, and the crowds poured in – more than fifty thousand of them – including for the first time the young Queen Elizabeth with her husband Prince Philip, and her sister Princess Margaret. Included in the list of competitors was a Major F. W. C. Weldon, Commander of the King's Troop, RHA, riding his own Liza Mandy, who had a bad fall over a drop fence of hazelwood bundles and put her rider in hospital. Fortunately, the experience spurred rather than dampened Frank Weldon's enthusiasm for the sport, and his subsequent success as an Olympic horseman and director of the Badminton event are a matter of glorious record. Lady riders again excelled at dressage, and there was a tremendous tussle on the final day for second place between Brigadier L. Bolton on Greylag and Brian Young on Dandy, who finally nudged ahead by just half a point after the show jumping. But the winner's trophy was presented by the Queen to Captain M. Darely, who slipped into the lead at the last minute on Emily Little to win with one of the few clear show jumping rounds of the day, finishing with 126.25, just two points ahead of Brian Young.

As for the Olympic hopefuls, when the team was finally announced after Badminton it heralded a major departure from the military dominance of the past. Reg Hindley and Bertie Hill were named as the first two civilians ever to represent Britain in equestrian events. Hill was to be mounted on John Miller's Stella, while Reg Hindley would ride his own Speculation, with Major Laurence Rook completing the trio on Starlight.

It was not an altogether happy Olympics. Bertie Hill eventually finished individual seventh and Reg Hindley was thirteenth, but the team had been well on its way to winning an Olympic medal when Laurence Rook took a crashing fall after Starlight had stumbled in a drainage ditch on the run in of the speed and endurance phase. Badly concussed, he remounted and finished the course, but in his confusion rode the wrong side of the marker flags, so the whole team was eliminated. It was a tragic end to four years of anticipation. Looking on the bright side, the British team had nevertheless shown themselves capable of equalling the European challenge. In no small way that was due to the Duke of Beaufort's generous and farsighted action in providing Badminton Park as a centre for British three-day eventing, and although that first programme in 1949 said that the 'sole purpose' of the competition was to prepare for the 1952 Games, there was no question that once the Olympics were over the competition at Badminton would come to an end. It had sown the seed for a whole new equestrian sport in Britain, prompted massive public support, and spawned a growing network of competitive one-day events. It was established as a championship in its own right, and would go on providing the main testing ground for Britain's assault on the major competitions of the world.

By way of consolidating that role, the following April Badminton was the venue of the European Championships. The British team of Bertie Hill, now paired with Bambi V, Reg Hindley on Speculation and the newly recruited Frank Weldon on his own brilliant Kilbarry, took the team gold medal, while Laurence Rook and Starlight, who had been left out of the team because of the horse's erratic performance, confounded their critics and delighted their supporters by taking the lead after the dressage, streaking across country and, in spite of a fence down in the show jumping ring, finishing the three days with the first ever plus score in the history of the event, clinching the title of individual European champion. It was a triumph, and British riders started a five-year run in which they would dominate the world.

At Badminton itself, the man who had built the very sound foundations on which a good measure of that success had blossomed, retired, and handed over the reins to Colonel Gordon Cox-Cox. Interestingly, while more and more civilians were flocking to the sport as competitors (and now totally dominate it), the administration remained very firmly in the hands of the military. Badminton committees and lists of officials were dominated for years by brigadiers, colonels, majors and captains. Only in the past few years has the balance swung from majors to misters, though the Army influence is still strong and the whole operation is still run with the precise planning and execution of a major military operation. So it is true to say that not only the Duke of Beaufort, but also the British Army made a valuable contribution to the establishment, development and indeed the very survival of Badminton in particular, and the sport of eventing in general.

Until the European Championships of 1953, Badminton was still the only *three*-day event in the country, supported by twelve one-day events. But in September a new three-day competition was staged in Yorkshire at Harewood House, acknowledging in its programme that 'The 1952 Games at Helsinki proved conclusively that the influence of the BHS and of Badminton has already become of decisive value. In staging these Harewood trials it is hoped to reinforce the success already achieved' – adding, with a note of optimism, and echoing the sentiments of 1949, 'the ultimate aim is to select a team which will win at the next Olympics' – which, of course, it did!

So by the early 1950s the sport was well established in Britain, whose riders were taking on the world, and winning. Badminton could to a certain extent shed some of the heavy responsibility of being the sole source of experience and settle down to consolidating its own role as a significant world class championship. It gradually became more difficult for riders to qualify for the competition. Originally, provided that you were British, a member of the BHS and over seventeen years of age, with a horse not older than ten, you were eligible. But as the course became more severe and the prestige of winning the Badminton Championship more acute, the organizers began to use the various one- and three-day events as a yardstick of competence. There was never any question that any of the subsequent three-day events, at Harewood, then Burghley and Wiley, would topple Badminton from its pre-eminent position. They were testing grounds for Badminton, which stood alone as the supreme test.

There were gradually fewer potted histories describing horses as 'a Government charger', or 'has hunted regularly with the so-and-so hunt' or 'Grade A show jumper, done well in working hunter classes', and more declaring success at the one-day events at Larkhill, Great Auclum, Wellesbourne, and so on. In 1957 the first new qualification demanded a place in the first five, or completion of the cross-country stage of two affiliated one-day events. Just four years later it went up a notch to 'completing the Open or Intermediate Class in two horse trials', though it was not until 1976 that the ruling insisted on a horse completing one three-day event, and its rider, two three-day events before they would even be considered. In

Top right: The Royals watching the vet's inspection.

Top left: Queen Elizabeth in the stand with Princess Margaret in 1952. On the right is Lady Beaufort and standing on the left is Lord Beaufort.

Bottom right: The Duke of Beaufort riding out with the Queen.

Above: The Queen Mother enjoying the informality of Badminton with Princess Margaret and the Duke of Beaufort in 1957.

fact the present director, Frank Weldon, admits candidly that he would like to see the qualifications for Badminton even tougher and more exclusive. As it is, the Badminton course itself is the final arbiter. Only the finest riders and horses ever complete the three days. Those who are not quite up to scratch never make it to the end of the second day.

As the sport has grown in stature so the riders and trainers have had to improve their own technique and ability to keep pace with the demands of more complex and technical courses. In that aspect of the sport Badminton has led the way on a steadily upward curve to the point where its cross-country course is now regarded as one of the toughest and most challenging in the world. In contrast, the story of dressage at Badminton has been one of fits and starts. After the initial flurry of flying changes and five-loop serpentines contained in the early test, it took a while for the ruling body of the sport to realize that event horses did not have to aspire to Grand Prix standards, but needed a test that would display the general obedience and suppleness of a horse whose main purpose in life was to complete the far more crucial stage of speed and endurance, and emerge fit enough on day three to perform a show jumping test. So in 1959 the test contained a more sensible combination of movements. But there were thirty of them, and the test took twelve minutes to perform instead of the original nine and a half, though the scoring was made a lot simpler, with each movement marked out of a maximum of six points. In 1963 the test was changed again. It was reduced to just seven and a half minutes, but still made the same basic demands on horse and rider through the sequence of movements. However, no doubt inspired by the increasing technicality of the cross-country fences, in 1973 the ruling body of the sport, the FEI, decided to make the dressage test more technical. Flying changes were back as part of a decidedly more complex test. There were howls of protest (though according to the etiquette of the sport very discreet howls!) and the dreaded test lasted just two years. In 1975 it was back to basics; and a test emerged that is still in use today.

Undoubtedly the greatest catalyst in Badminton's history has been Frank Weldon, who took over as course builder in 1965, becoming director in 1967. His influence on the administration and prestige of the event through the development of the course are described in detail in Chapter 4. So many of his achievements have taken place behind the scenes, affecting the organization, and the competitors, that the impact of his decisions has seldom been immediately obvious to the public. However, on taking over in 1967 two of his decisions had an immediate effect on the 'look' of Badminton. First to go were the showing classes, which were held throughout Saturday. They took up valuable space and manpower, and were frankly a distraction to the main spectacle of the day – the cross-country. In the same year he abandoned the Little Badminton event. This had started in 1960 when the numbers of competitors had grown to such an extent that it was impossible to do all the dressage on one day. As Master (as the then Duke of Beaufort was always known) was not keen for the event to last more than three days, the only way to accommodate the growing numbers was to run two dressage arenas. As there was no guarantee that the two sets of judges would mark to the same standard, there was no way that the two sets of dressage marks could count towards the final score in the same competition. So although every competitor rode over the same cross-country course and the same show jumping fences, the Little Badminton competition took the 'overspill' of competitors. Some riders

The Olympic Games Three Day Event Team of 1956 in training at Porlock.
From left to right, Kilbarry (Lt.-Col. F. Weldon), Countryman III
(Mr Bertie Hill) and Starlight XV (Major L. Rook).

enjoyed the less pressurized atmosphere that somehow prevailed over the 'Little' competition, but it was generally unpopular with competitors who felt like second class citizens – somehow apart from the main championship. As a competitor himself Weldon had great sympathy for that argument, and scrapped the competition after 1965. He admits that it was not a straightforward decision. First he had to persuade Master to allow the dressage to run over two days. 'It was a bit like water dripping on stone,' he says. 'I just had to slip the idea to him gently that I might need to do a few extra dressage tests on the Wednesday morning, and once he'd got used to that idea it wasn't too difficult to take over the whole day.'

Frank Weldon admits that, although the Duke was still proud to have played such a key role in establishing the sport in Britain, as the competition grew he became less and less enchanted with the growing number of spectators who flooded his Park each year. As a result, in 1975 the pattern that had been set in the early 1960s of having the speed and endurance on Saturday, when most people could attend, was abruptly changed. Everything moved forward a day, making Friday the most important day of the competition, with show jumping on the Saturday. The Badminton office received floods of complaints from people all over the country who had to work on Fridays and did not want to miss the most exciting part of the event. This, of course, was exactly what the Duke wanted, as it reduced the numbers considerably. However, it was not just the great British public who were put out by the change. Her Majesty the Queen, by now a regular visitor to the event, also found the change disruptive to her routine, and after a gentle hint to the Duke the event was restored to the more convenient timetable of dressage on Thursday and Friday, with Saturday still one of the biggest crowd pullers in Britain's sporting calendar.

One of the more recent developments to change the character of the event happened in 1982, when the tradition of running a BSJA show jumping event on the Sunday afternoon, after the final round of the championships, was abandoned. Over the years the Sunday competition had played host to the greatest names in show jumping, and in the early years, when the infant sport of eventing needed all the support it could get, the added attraction of show jumping on the final day helped to bring in the crowds. But by the late 1970s the Badminton Championship was more than capable of standing on its own. Besides, Frank Weldon was convinced that, once the Queen had presented the Whitbread Trophy to the winner of the championship, most people simply wanted to get in their cars and head for home.

In addition to the almost monumental effect of Frank Weldon's presence at Badminton, a number of individual competitors have helped to shape the popularity and character of the event. From the very beginning the public have flocked to Badminton to see their 'star' riders and equally famous horses. In the mid 1950s it was the triumphant Olympic team of Hill, Rook and Weldon, while the end of that decade was dominated by the young Sheila Willcox. With her great horses, High and Mighty and Airs and Graces, she was the darling of the public in her winning years of 1957, 1958 and 1959 – the Lucinda Green and Virginia Holgate of her day. In the early 1960s it was Anneli Drummond-Hay and her classic mount Merely-a-Monarch who stole the public's heart, while from 1967 onwards the World, European and Olympic champions once again fired the public imagination – riders like Richard Meade and Mark Phillips, Jane Bullen with her gallant little Olympic horse Our Nobby, and of course the remarkable, record breaking Lucinda Prior-Palmer (now Green) with six Badminton championships to her name and a whole string of World and European titles. But winners apart, perhaps the one person who did more in the mid 1970s to boost not just Badminton but the sport in general, was HRH the Princess Anne. She made her first appearance in 1971, riding her own Doublet. The Badminton box office had a sudden surge of applications for tickets from people who had probably never been near a three-day event in their lives, and on cross-country day the crowds were swollen by the royal watchers anxious to see the Princess in action. In the country as a whole thousands of little girls were suddenly eventing mad, wanting to emulate the participation and success of the royal competitor in one of the most demanding of all equestrian sports. Princess Anne herself is very diffident about her influence at that time, saying: 'I remember turning up there wondering what on earth I was doing. It all seemed very far above my humble exploits up until then.' But clearly the faith of her trainer, Alison Oliver, was not misplaced, as the Princess and Doublet finished fifth, and went on later that year to become European champions.

Despite its growth in popularity, eventing has not gone the way of its equestrian 'cousin' show jumping, and become a professional sport.

Badminton's top price of £6,000 in 1986 is still the highest purse in the sport, and

*Lucinda Green (née Prior Palmer), the
most successful rider ever at Badminton
was first and third in 1977 riding
George and Killaire.*

well outstripped by prize money available to show jumpers. But while the Smiths and Whittakers of this world are able to enter their top jumpers in dozens of competitions throughout a season, a top class eventer would never want to do more than one Badminton a year. And yet it is an increasingly expensive sport, in time as well as money. Those riders who want to do well at Badminton and other major international events have to devote the majority of their time to riding, if they are to reach the peak of ability that is now demanded. It is a rare horseman these days who can work five days a week and fit in serious competitive riding as a hobby in his or her spare time. Fortunately, they're not a totally defunct breed. It's their guts and enthusiasm for the sport that is its life blood and maintains the 'hats over the windmills' atmosphere at every competition. But more and more riders are finding that to stay at the top they need not just one, or even two horses, but often a whole string of animals to maintain a continuity from the most novice of one-day events through to the championship demands of Badminton. Sponsorship has gone some way towards providing the answer, with major companies seeing an opportunity to advertise their name while 'leasing' the horses in their ownership to world class riders.

One of the first to latch on to the idea was rider Vincent Jones, who ran the horse Bleak Hills in the ownership of his own company Precispark Limited in 1975. Three years later Lucinda Green became the first British eventer to secure major sponsorship with Overseas Containers Limited. That was followed in 1980 by Richard Meade's deal with the builders George Wimpey and Mark Phillips' association with Range Rover. It did not take long for the idea to mushroom. In 1986 nineteen of the Badminton competitors were sponsored, with many more companies supporting riders who did not enter. There is no doubt that the money and support offered by these commercial benefactors has helped to keep British riders in contention for top honours, but Frank Weldon sounds a note of caution. 'Too many of the young riders are looking for a sponsor as soon as they've had just a little bit of success. They seem to regard it as a right, rather than something to be earned.' And while he accepts that in today's competitive climate it is just not possible for a rider to emulate his own glorious record with one top horse, he would clearly hate to see the dedication and spirit of the individual lost in the scramble for commercial dependence.

For whatever else Badminton may become as a major public spectacle, and even as a vehicle for the ad men of Whitbreads, at the end of the day it remains a supreme trial of outstanding partnership and athletic ability that is won by the courage and skill of an individual horse and rider. The money may help with the training and smooth the path to the bank, but after that they are on their own.

Winning an Olympic medal is still every athlete's dream and ultimate goal. The national pride and achievement it represents is incomparable. But in eventing a win at Badminton is in the same league. Over almost forty years it has become the competition every event rider in the world wants to win – which is not a bad reputation for something that began life as a 'warm-up' to the main attraction and which the director Frank Weldon still refers to as 'our little gymkhana'!

Right: Helen Ogden on Cressage 1986.
Overleaf: Ian Stark on Sir Wattie in 1984.

3

THE COURSE

If you drive through the Badminton estate along the narrow lane that leads to Luckington Village in the late summer or early autumn, it is quite likely that you will see a battered old Land Rover parked under a tree, its driver staring stoically into space or pacing round in circles muttering to himself. There is nothing particularly sinister or surprising about either of these activities, for the man is Colonel Frank Weldon, and the staring and mutterings are an essential ingredient in the process of designing the cross-country phase of Badminton's Whitbread Championship.

Every year since 1965 Frank Weldon's fences have offered the ultimate test of horsemanship in the world. For the past twenty years there has never been a European, World, or even Olympic course to challenge Badminton's reputation as an arena for excellence. And that is due entirely to what the riders unanimously label as Weldon's 'genius', and what commentator Raymond Brookes-Ward says is his 'courage, and unique creative ability to put up fences that everybody says are impossible to jump, which frighten the living daylights out of riders, and yet still produce the results'.

There is no event rider in the world who does not want to win the Badminton title, for such is the prestige of the event that it now ranks alongside an Olympic gold medal in terms of individual achievement. Every one of Britain's top riders will tell you that it is because they have met the challenge of Badminton that they have the confidence to attack any other course, anywhere in the world. This is precisely what the Duke of Beaufort wanted to achieve when he offered the Park for its first competition in 1949. Not that those early courses stand true comparison with today's obstacles. Like every other sporting activity, eventing has made more demands on its competitors as results have gradually pushed back the barriers of achievement. Horses do not run any faster nor jump any higher or longer than they did thirty or more years ago, but their riders have become more skilful at meeting the demands of increasingly ingenious course builders. The original director and course builder at Badminton, Colonel Trevor Horn, would be the first to admit that when the sport took its first faltering steps in the spring of 1949 he did not know the first thing about designing cross-country fences beyond what he had learned during his two-week involvement with the 1948 Olympics at Aldershot and his experiences over natural obstacles out hunting.

The earliest programmes have neither a map of the course nor a list of fences, so it is difficult to know exactly what they looked like. But John Shedden, the event's first winner on Golden Willow, remembers them as being 'lovely big fences – the sort you could really ride at'. His description was backed up by one of the early fence judges, who recalls the course as being 'on-going and galloping. There were none of the technical, combination fences we get nowadays, where riders need to control and steer their horses through. It was such a joy to watch horses like Starlight and Kilbarry or High and Mighty just galloping on, never breaking stride as the fences just disappeared behind them.'

It was 1952, Olympic year, before the organizers thought to include a list of the fences in the official programme, and from that we can see that Trevor Horn rarely took his obstacles to the maximum height of 3 ft 11 in. Most fences were 3 ft 6 in or 3 ft 9 in, with only fence 16, a Park Post and Rails, up to maximum height. They did, however, have an amazing 6 ft sheer drop into the Quarry. The Coffin – described by Frank Weldon as 'the graveyard of so many hopes and ambitions' – had just a 2 ft fence in, to a 4 ft 6 in ditch, with a 3 ft rail out. In comparison, the dimensions of Weldon's Horse Trials Support Groups Coffin in 1986 were rails of 3 ft 6 and 3 ft 11 – which illustrates why so many early riders agree that the courses they were jumping were possibly somewhat less demanding than the present Pony Club Championships. The obstacles did nevertheless call for great courage and skill from the competitors: most riders came straight to Badminton from a season's hunting, with none of the months, even years of preparation needed now. Many came to grief at the Coffin, small though it was, because the hunting types were just not used to slowing down on the approach and controlling their horses through the elements. Experienced horsemen such as John Shedden and Olympic rider Laurence Rook coped more easily with the trickier fences, while the big island fences suited their bold galloping horses perfectly. Both men admit to being run away with on the course, Rook when riding Starlight, who one year took the ditch, the stone-faced bank *and* the lane in one leap at the old Luckington Lane crossing, while Shedden's horse, Golden Willow, flew the Irish Bank in one without touching down, a distance later measured at some 36 ft. A remarkable jump in itself, but even more so when you realize that Willow was ridden in a standing martingale and gag snaffle, which should have checked his stride and exuberance.

Apart from their actual dimensions, the fences would also seem less impressive to modern eyes because the timbers used were much smaller. Early photographs show relatively spindly poles compared with the massive tree trunks that are a hallmark of Weldon's fences. Charlie Chappell, the old Duke's head forester, who actually helped to build Trevor Horn's courses, put it this way: 'When I was working on the course we used to be able to hold the pole with one hand and hammer in a nail with the other. Now you need two men just to lift the timbers up, and sometimes even a JCB!'

The other main difference between those early courses and the ones we are now familiar with is the route taken by the riders. The roads and tracks course

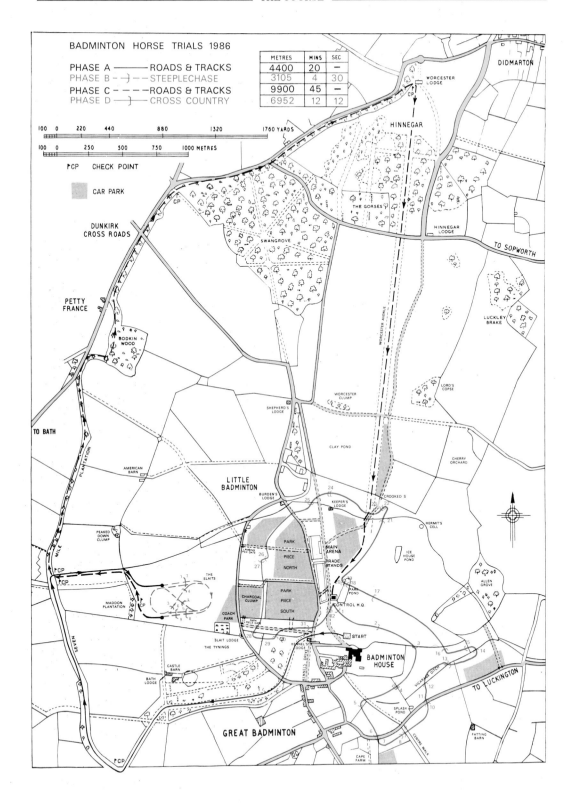

originally went out of the Park and over the main A433 to Didmarton, where the steeplechase phase was run over the old Chase Course behind the village. Once back in the Park, the cross-country course began just to the right of the lake, circled down over the Vicarage Fields to Cape Farm (the present location of Tom Smith's Walls), then turned left in front of Badminton House and continued behind the Kennel Lodge, into the woods in front of Bath Lodge, before turning right-handed again to come back across the main village road and finish just north of the lake, by the side of the water but not in it. It was not until 1956, by which time Lt.-Col. R. B. 'Babe' Moseley and Lt.-Col. G. G. Cox-Cox had taken over as joint organizers, that the lake featured as the last fence, and the steeplechase phase was moved to its present site. Until 1966 there was also a Phase E to accommodate – a 'run in' of some 1400 yards to be ridden immediately after jumping the last fence. In theory this was a chance to 'let the horse down' after a flat-out gallop over the fences. In practice it used up valuable stamina needed for Phase D, and was dropped in 1967 when the 'new guard' took over at Badminton under Frank Weldon's directorship and Laurence Rook, heading strong British opposition, persuaded the FEI to change its rules.

With only minimal television coverage, and still relatively few spectators, the Badminton course did not need to be a compact unit with fences grouped to give easy access and viewing to the public. It rambled over the four-mile course and riders needed to keep their wits about them to follow the route, which was rather scantily marked by yellow bunting at the start and finish of each phase, and had yellow discs, flags or pieces of paper to mark the boundaries and changes of direction.

The course was not roped off until about 1970, so riders could take whatever direction they liked between fences, as long as they jumped them in order. If they

Left: Frank Weldon performing his dressage test on Kilbarry in 1954.
Right: Col. Moseley (left) with Col. G. Cox-Cox standing next to one of the cross country jumps in 1964.

found a short cut between obstacles that would save them valuable seconds, it was perfectly all right to take that line. In theory riders can still choose their own route between fences if they think they can see a quicker line, but as they would never get through the huge crowds it would be a futile exercise. Throughout the 1950s, though, there were no such complications, and riders revelled in the challenge of outwitting the course designer to find precious time-cutting alternatives. Laurence Rook recalls galloping through one of the rhododendron clumps and startling a spectator who thought he had found a quiet spot to relieve himself. John Shedden was once caught in the act of marking a route through the trees in the wood near Bath Lodge by the old Duke and the Queen. He was cutting notches in the bark to signpost a short cut from the old Quarry fence when he bumped into Master, walking the course with the young queen. 'Master was most amused, and warned me to watch out for the big holes of a badgers' set. But when I actually rode the course it wasn't the holes I had to watch for, but the public. Some spectators saw my marks and thought they were a path for them to follow, so when I came thundering out of the Quarry there they were walking down my little path. I gave a yell, there was a hell of a scramble and everyone scattered. That was the fun of it, you had to use your brain.'

Young Sheila Willcox caught on to this very quickly. By the time she was competing, in the late 1950s, the crowds were increasing, and although the course itself was still open, many of the fences were roped to keep spectators away from the takeoffs and landings. This did not deter the young rider, who was quite determined to find the quickest way round the course. It was again at the Quarry that she threw the fence judges and stewards into confusion by leaving the marked area on the landing side of the fence and setting off through the car park. 'I'd worked it all out beforehand with the attendants,' she says, 'and knew exactly where the cars would be and where I could get out back onto the course. My route was risky, but much quicker than the one on the map. And it was fun to be able to outwit them.'

One of the spectators just arriving by car, who was dumbfounded to see Sheila galloping among the vehicles, was the young Lucinda Prior-Palmer on her first visit to the event. Her own subsequent speed and daring have made her the most successful competitor at Badminton in the event's history. Perhaps riders would still be looking for alternative routes out of that fence if it were not for the fact that in 1961 Master declared the woods at Bath Lodge out of bounds, as the horses were disturbing the vixens and their cubs, and as hunting was virtually Master's religion the needs of the foxes came before any consideration for the course.

There is no doubt that the Badminton event had achieved its general goal of helping to produce champions, and specifically to find riders and horses suitable for training as a team to compete at the Olympic Games in Helsinki in 1952. As it turned out, 1952 was not to be a glorious year, but Britain did win both a team gold and an individual bronze in the Stockholm Olympics of 1956, and took the team and individual gold medals at the European Championships in 1953, 1954, 1955 and 1957. A quite remarkable five-year record, fuelled by the challenge of Badminton's annual trial over its Olympic Horse Trials course. But for ten years after that British teams did not win a single international competition. Captain J. Templar salvaged national pride somewhat by taking the individual gold medal on M'Lord Connolly in 1962, when the European Championships were held at Burghley, but apart from that it was a barren decade, with the ultimate ignominy coming in 1964 when the British were eliminated from the Tokyo Olympics.

It has to be said that if Badminton can claim the lion's share of credit for creating an atmosphere and arena in which to prepare British riders for international success, it must also share in the blame for the decline in the years following 1958. Gordon Cox-Cox and 'Babe' Moseley worked together as director and deputy for ten years from 1954. Although both men were distinguished cavalry officers, and Moseley was a champion amateur National Hunt jockey, neither man had ever actually ridden in a three-day event. Their knowledge was bound to be somewhat limited. While the rest of the world took a leaf from Britain's book and provided tests at home to sharpen the performance of their riders, at Badminton fences were still not up to maximum height, and it became quite common to hear spectators commenting disdainfully, 'We jump bigger stuff than that out hunting'. As international success continued to elude the British, interest in the sport declined. There was still a hard core of support, of course, among dedicated riders and spectators, but attendance at Badminton started to fall, the BHS began losing money, and the cross-country fences on the premier championship course were simply not offering the sort of challenge that could set the sport alight and rekindle the flame of those glorious five golden years. Even in that Olympic year of 1964, when you would have expected Badminton to provide a stiffer challenge to prepare riders for the competition, none of Badminton's fences were up to maximum height. Only four of the thirty-four obstacles stood at 3 ft 10 in, while most were straightforward island fences ranging from 3 ft 6 in to 3 ft 9 in – hardly a test of Olympic proportions.

There is no doubt that 1964 was a watershed for Badminton. Things could hardly have been worse for the sport, administratively and competitively. It was logical to

Above: In 1952 the dressage arena looked like this from the top of Badminton House. Spectators could watch from their cars or sitting on benches and straw bales. The tented shopping area and stands are at top right, show jumping ring top centre and the lake can be seen top left.
Right: The shape of the steeplechase course altered in 1980 with a figure 8 instead of a circle.

assume, therefore, that if eventing was to survive at all, things could only get better. And they did. The Duke's heir, David Somerset, was made chairman. Admitting that he would have to give most of his time to his own business commitments in London, and having not the slightest interest in building cross-country courses, he had the courage and wisdom, against great opposition, to appoint Frank Weldon as course builder for the 1965 event.

Weldon was an inspired choice. His reputation as an international horseman was impeccable, he had seen the fences at most major international three-day events since 1953, either as a competitor or as an official delegate, and he had been applying his knowledge of course design to Pony Club competitions for several years. Like others, he had been dismayed to see the Badminton cross-country course 'geared down to the lowest common denominator', and the effect that this was having on Britain's international performance. He just could not wait to get his hands on the fences. His approach was simple: 'It was very much a chicken and egg situation. I knew that Badminton had to pull its socks up if we wanted to start producing international champions, and the thing that would perk Badminton up was for us to start winning abroad again, because everybody wants to be on the winning side.'

Weldon began as he intended to continue. Virtually every fence on the course in 1965 was bigger. Eight of them were put up to maximum height, and none of the island fences was less than 3 ft 8 in. The rails in and out of the Coffin were unchanged at 3 ft 3 in., but regular competitors were shocked to find fences like the first Luckington Lane crossing up from 3 ft 4 in to 3 ft 9 in, the Post and Rails at the maximum 3 ft 11 in instead of 3 ft 6 in, a sponsor's fence, the brightly coloured Whitbread Pocket (the first time the event's sponsors had been mentioned on the course) standing 3 ft 10 in high and 4 ft 6 in wide just one fence from home, with the final obstacle, the log into the lake, up 4 in to 3 ft 8 in. Weldon was absolutely determined that 'never again would British riders go abroad and be beaten'. His own experience as a rider had shown how much bigger and more difficult the foreign courses could be. 'So I started right away by making Badminton much bigger, because I realized we would never be any good internationally unless things were right at home. When you go abroad all events are different, and it can be alarming when the language is different, the smells are different. But if you can walk around the course and say: "Well, I jumped that, or something like it, last year at Badminton," then you're absolutely confident about how your horse is going to run across country, and you start with an enormous advantage.'

And it can surely be no coincidence that within two years of Weldon taking over as course builder at Badminton, Britain broke its losing run and started to pick up international honours.

In 1966 the event was cancelled after a week of torrential rain. The small gully in the Vicarage Ditch was a raging torrent, and much of the Park was flooded. Because the decision to cancel was not taken until the day before the competitors' briefing, everyone had arrived, including the intrepid Irish and French teams. After walking the course the French declared they were rather pleased the event had been cancelled, as they would not have to face Weldon's course, which included many new fences, such as the horrific looking Shark's Teeth; a combination of three fences in Huntsman's Close that offered a 'bounce' stride – quite common in show jumping by then, but very new to horse trials; the first combination fence that

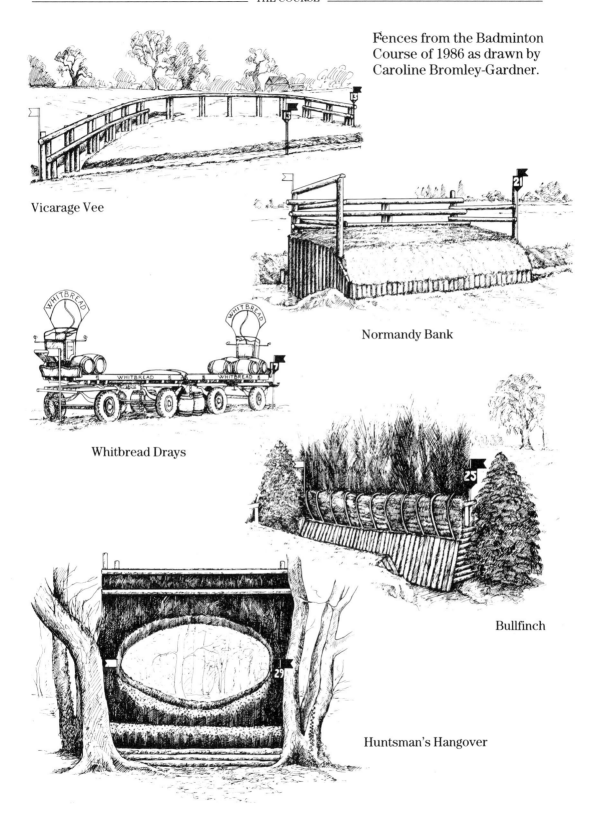

Fences from the Badminton Course of 1986 as drawn by Caroline Bromley-Gardner.

Vicarage Vee

Normandy Bank

Whitbread Drays

Bullfinch

Huntsman's Hangover

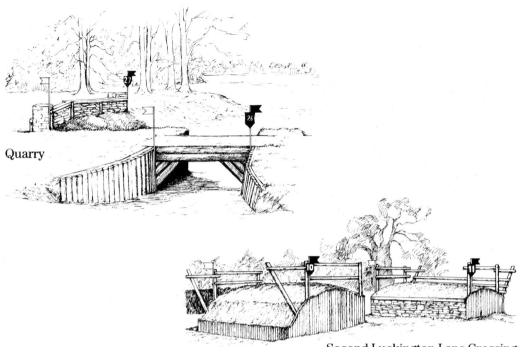

Quarry

Second Luckington Lane Crossing

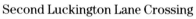

Cross Question

Whitbread Bar

Lamb Creep

offered alternative routes, called the Cattle Crush; and a number of other obstacles that were all dimensionally and visually far more exciting than anything that had ever appeared there before. The following year Weldon, who had now officially become director of Badminton, offered exactly the same course of big, impressive fences, which provided the perfect overture for British riders and horses, who went on to clinch the European gold at Punchestown that autumn.

Badminton in Olympic year 1968 was a real champion's challenge. Jane Bullen (now Holderness-Roddam) on Our Nobby won the event and went on to help win the team gold at the Mexico Olympics in the company of Major Derek Allhusen on Lochinvar, Richard Meade on Cornishman, and Sgt Ben Jones riding The Poacher, with the Allhusen–Lochinvar partnership taking the individual silver. Britain was back on winning form, in the first division of the sport, and has stayed there ever since.

Weldon's formula is simple. His often quoted dogma that 'I build fences to frighten the life out of the riders, but not hurt the horses' means that over the years his flair and originality, coupled with an innate sense for the capabilities of a really fit horse, have produced cross-country courses that have become the most exciting, demanding and prestigious test of both horse and rider in the world.

Many of the fences evolve from the natural features and contours of the park, and some have been around in one form or another since the very first year. The Luckington Lane fences and Tom Smith's Walls at Cape Farm are obvious examples, with the Vicarage Ditch and ha-ha offering plenty of scope over which to build fences like the Vicarage Vee, The Stockholm and the Pardubice Taxis. Nowadays, the lake provides one of the most spectacular fences on the course.

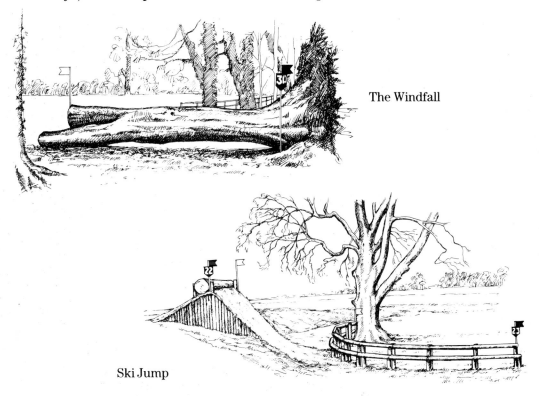

The Windfall

Ski Jump

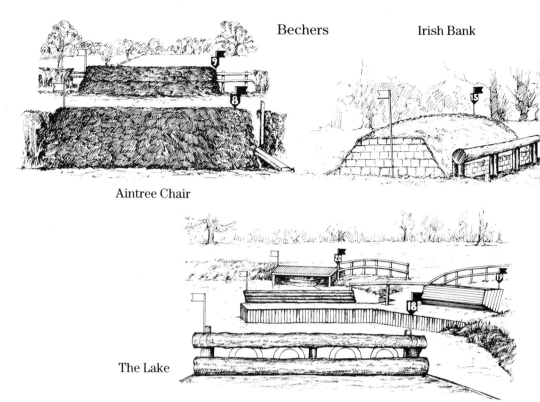

Bechers   Irish Bank

Aintree Chair

The Lake

Early directors thought it was unfair to put a water jump in the middle of the course in case competitors fell off and had to complete the rest of the course soaking wet. Weldon had no such reservations, and in 1969 made the lake fences the half way markers, where they have stayed ever since. The familiar jump in and out of the water at the north end of the lake was given added spice in 1985 when the drought of the previous summer made the water table so low that Weldon, with his course builders Alan Willis and Gilbert Thornbury, could construct a jetty half way across the lake and add a third element to the combination. This caused havoc the first year, with what Weldon agrees were 'far too many eliminations'. But he is determined that British riders should get used to the triple element in the water so they do not get caught out by it on foreign courses – so it will remain a regular feature until the competitors are, quite literally, taking it in their stride.

Most of the complex combination fences, which are usually located on the flat of the Vicarage fields where there are no natural contours to help, have come from Weldon's own imagination. The Catherine Wheel, the Chevrons and the Brandy Glass are all examples of 'an evening spent at home with graph paper and a glass of whisky', while some of the most spectacular and famous obstacles have been adapted from fences that have caught Weldon's eye at major international competitions over the past thirty years, 'from here to Singapore'.

Unlike many course designers, Weldon always gives credit to a fence's origins, no matter how much he may alter the original concept – hence fences with names such as the Cirencester Rails from the Midland Bank Championship, the Helsinki Steps from the Olympics, and perhaps the most famous of his adaptations, the Normandy Bank. It first appeared in 1970, the year following the championships at

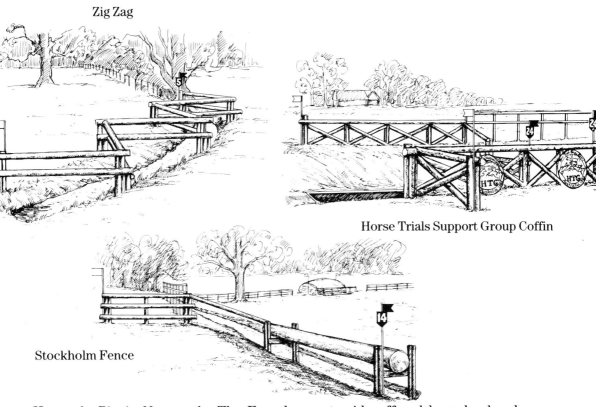

Zig Zag

Horse Trials Support Group Coffin

Stockholm Fence

Haras du Pin in Normandy. The French countryside offered huge banks above ditches, which the French course designer had included in the cross-country section, adhering to the rule that obstacles must represent, as far as possible, the natural features of the land. While the prizes were being presented after the event – which the British team had won – Weldon was half a mile away, tape measure in hand, working out the dimensions, 'as I was pretty sure I could reproduce the idea back at Badminton'. He goes on to describe what he did in the Park as 'just showing how artificially you could create a pimple in the middle of nowhere'. The 'pimple' emerged as a bank 3 ft 9 in high, with a 2 ft 3 in rail on the edge (it is now at 3 ft) and a yawning ditch on the landing side. The fence caused a sensation, and as Weldon tells it, 'Everyone was convinced that I was a lunatic and out to kill them. For the first five years it was around, you couldn't get near the fence for spectators.' In fact one horse was killed at the Bank, an Irish horse, one of only three fatal casualties in the history of Badminton. Weldon maintains that accidents usually only happen when horses are unfit or badly ridden (though some just have unlucky or awkward landings), and that a fit, boldly ridden horse will never come to grief at his obstacles. His belief is borne out in practice by watching the many fluid combinations of horse and rider who make even the most impossible looking jumps seem relatively straightforward. As far as the Normandy Bank was concerned, riders soon got into the rhythm of the jump, leaping onto the bank and going straight over the rails without trying to put in a short stride, then powering out over the rails to clear the ditch with yards to spare. As Mark Phillips recalls: 'Some of us had jumped the similar fence in France, so we knew we could do it,' and very soon the rest of Britain's riders picked up that confidence, so that now, as

Weldon says, 'People walk straight past the Normandy Bank without giving it a second glance'.

In 1982 there were gasps of dismay when the Horsens Bridge appeared – a footbridge over the ha-ha ending in a 2 ft 6 in set of rails with a 13 ft spread over the ditch to the landing side. The late Martin Whiteley, a member of the Committee of Appeal in 1981, was heard to remark that he did think 'Frank should have filled in the hole underneath'. Weldon's reaction was typically uncompromising. 'The whole point of the fence was to have this cavern which the horses just stepped out over: the object of the exercise was to make the heart flutter. And now, nobody bothers about it.' And again, in 1984 when the Frauenfeld Platform appeared as part of the Quarry complex, there were raised eyebrows and hearts in mouths as riders negotiated a leap onto a wide, bridge-like construction that was 3 ft 9 in high and 9 ft 2 in across. 'But I'll bet you sixpence from now on no one will take any notice,' is what he said before the event in 1986 – and he was right.

Nevertheless there are times when Weldon sails pretty close to the wind, in a sport where the line between the bold, jumpable fence and the grief-maker is paper thin. Lucinda Green thinks he goes 'nearer the brink than anyone else in the world' but still rates him as the best there is. 'I really would apply the word "genius" to him,' she says. 'He really does petrify us, you can never grow complacent with Frank.' Her approach is to see the competition as a contest, a battle of wills if you like, between herself and the course builder. 'It was in 1978,' she recalls, 'when I was riding Village Gossip – he was brilliant, but I was still at odds with him, and very worried about the course. On the night before the cross-country my mother slipped a note under my door simply saying, "You're OK, you'll manage – don't forget it's you against the course builder, nothing else." I'd never thought of it that way before, and suddenly I thought, "Oh yes, lovely, that will give me a bit of a challenge. I'll jolly well show you that I can jump your fences." She'd given me something to hang on to when I needed it most. Now in other competitions I sometimes think, "Right, you smart so-and-so course builder, we're going to have a fight on this," and it makes the whole thing much more fun.' This is especially true when the riders manage to outwit Weldon, as they did in 1983 over the Footbridge, which straddled a natural ditch two fences after the Whitbread Drays. Weldon had worked out four possible routes: a quick way, jumping diagonally across the bridge and the ditch, and three longer routes, each very time-consuming. The riders found a fifth alternative that was very easy, and only fractionally slower than the quick route. Weldon was furious, but had to admit that he had been outwitted, and vowed, 'They won't do that to me again.'

It's what Mark Phillips calls 'the cumulative effect' of Weldon's courses that in his opinion 'sort the men from the boys'. 'In a good year the fences just flow, and really it's a joy to ride the course. But there have been years, like 1973, when there wasn't a single fence that was really bad or big, but the horses were constantly landing on rising ground, so by the time they got to the Keeper's Rails they were stopping. There was nothing particularly unjumpable about the rail, but because of the cumulative effect of what had gone before, they got that far and then said, "I've had enough".' He accepts that in those circumstances it is up to the rider not to 'heap trouble on the horse, by finding the best solution when you're walking the course'. A ploy he has often used, if he has been worried about a particular fence, is to 'catch Frank in a quiet moment, say at the cocktail party, and ask his advice. He's

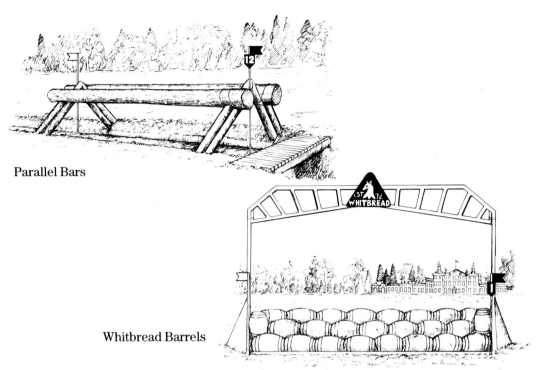

Parallel Bars

Whitbread Barrels

such a good barometer that if I say, "Perhaps I'll take the long way there", or suggest a particular route, and he says, "You could be right," then you know for certain you're right, and to leave the other routes well alone.' This is assuming that his so-called 'easier' alternatives can take the sting out of some of the obstacles. As Phillips says, 'Whenever Frank asks a really big question at a fence, if you care to take your time there's always an escape hatch'. The course of 1985 was nevertheless in his opinion 'the biggest, most difficult Badminton I've ever seen, where the options were almost more difficult than the direct routes', and this four times winner of the event admitted that for once he was 'almost glad I didn't have a horse that year, and wasn't able to compete'. You'll rarely get Weldon to admit that he has made a mistake, and he says staunchly, 'I'll defend myself against all comers', standing by the decisions he has made and pointing to the successful riders who have completed the course and proved his point. Raymond Brookes-Ward says it is always easy to tell when Frank begins to get worried by the way things are going because he gets through at least forty cigarettes in a day instead of his usual ten.

Occasionally he will admit to a miscalculation. 'Now and again,' he confesses, 'I do wish perhaps I'd made it a bit easier for the rider. In 1985, for instance, there were too many eliminations at the water.' That was the first year of the 'bounce' over the jetty – something that has been a feature of European courses for some time. 'I suppose I should have realized the amount of alarm and dispondency it would cause appearing there for the first time – but give it a few years and it'll be fine.' That's the sort of comment that sends trainers scurrying to their own schooling courses to prepare riders for Weldon's annual test. Lars Sederholm, who has trained dozens of successful Badminton riders, including the 1969 winner Richard Walker on Pasha, admits that he, and many other trainers, had to change their views about preparing event horses and riders in the mid 1960s when Weldon's 'related distances' became a regular feature of horse trials. 'It used to be just a question of getting the horses going in fourth gear, and perhaps concentrating on getting them over a problem fence. Suddenly it all required much more finesse and control, and we had to get this across to those riders who wanted to ride at the problem fences as they had done in the old days, with speed and verve as if there was no tomorrow.'

Preparing each year's course is practically a twelve-month operation. There are weeks of thinking and planning as Weldon tries to visualize the completely new fences against the existing landscape, and to plot ways of altering some of the more established landmarks as the course changes direction each year. In September Alan Willis, who has worked with Frank Weldon since 1966, and his colleague Gilbert Thornbury begin work on the director's grand plan. They start with the ground work, returfing the banks, clearing out and making good the sides of ditches, and doing the major earth-moving work where artificial ditches or banks have to be created for fences such as the Normandy Bank, the Coffin, the Ski Jump and the Frauenfeld Platform. Several years ago Weldon hit on the idea of using 'skelpings', a particularly rough chipping hewn out of local quarries, to improve the drainage on the takeoff and landing sites of each fence. The skelpings are laid under the surface on each side of the fence and then turfed over. By the time the event comes round in April the grass is well settled, and when it rains (as it often does) the ground stays well drained, giving a firm footing just where the horses need it most. Several years ago the dressage arena in the main ring was treated in the same way to ensure reasonable going for the tests regardless of the weather.

Badminton is the only international event in the world that builds its fences from wood grown on its own estate. The trees are cut in October, mostly larch, each timber a standard 18 ft long, and 10 in in diameter. When Weldon took over the course in 1965 they were still digging the holes for the posts by hand with a pick and shovel, and sawing the timbers with a band saw. 'I brought them out of the Middle Ages,' he chuckles, 'by getting them to use machines and a chain saw.' He also revolutionized the construction of the fences. Originally they were held together by bolts, with wire wrapped around the uprights to give extra stability. But Weldon, who is no mean carpenter himself, devised a system in which the parallel poles are 'rested' on top of blocks of wood attached to the uprights, and then lashed into place with rope. If a horse gets trapped or caught up on a fence the ropes can quickly be slashed with an axe and the fence dismantled within seconds to release the animal. As the fence has not been destroyed it is then a fairly simple matter to rebuild it for the next competitor. This system has now been copied at most of the other major international competitions, who have seen its effectiveness in Gloucestershire. For the more complicated fences, such as the Catherine Wheel or the Chevrons, Weldon traces the outline on the ground using wooden pegs and string, but usually the fences are built, remodelled or updated just by a spoken instruction or the use of simple drawings.

Weldon spends most of the winter working on site with his men, preferring to leave the office work to his brother-in-law, Major Dyson, and the secretary, Jane Gundry, while he watches his creations develop stage by stage into realities. It can take anything from a few days to several weeks to construct a fence, depending on its complexity. Their deadline is the day before the competitors' briefing, when the ground jury carries out its inspection. By then the fences have to look exactly as

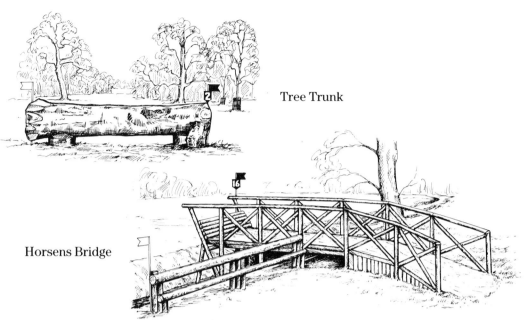

Tree Trunk

Horsens Bridge

they will be presented to the rider, complete with marker flags and any artificial decorations. The nine steeplechase fences are relatively easy to prepare, as Alan Willis's predecessor, George Stoneham, devised a set of portable jumps, built into frames that could be stored throughout the year, and put in place the week before the competiton. They need a certain amount of maintenance each year, but they never have to be built from scratch. This is another of Badminton's innovations that have been copied elsewhere.

While each year Frank Weldon gives his course a new look with inventive and challenging fences, one thing that he cannot change are the dimensions. 'The effect I achieve is purely psychological,' he says, 'and this is what I play on. You can't build jumps that are going to impress people by their size because the limit is 3 ft 11 in high and 5 ft 11 in wide, which is well within the capability of the average horse. Child's play.' Of course what Weldon realized years ago is that it is not the size of the fence that counts so much as where you put it, and while a 3 ft 6 in fence may look nothing on the flat, put it on the side of a slope, at the top of a ramp or in a gully and it can be devastating. He maintains that, 'In this country we produce the finest horses in the world for eventing and there are no better riders than you'll find in Britain. So what I set out to do is test the rider.' Which he unfailingly does, year after year. As Olympic Champion and Badminton winner Mark Todd says, 'On any other course in the world you'd get to a fence the size of the Whitbread Drays (3 ft 11 in high with a 5 ft 6 in spread) and you'd think it was a big fence, but at Badminton you're just glad to jump it because it's one of the easier fences on the course.'

Many people ask Frank Weldon if he ever gets a horse to try out the fences before the competition to make sure they will work and that his judgement is right. Certainly in the very early days Master would often gallop over a few of the less imposing fences on his hunter, and Ronnie Dallas, secretary to the Beaufort Hunt and the man in charge of stabling for the event, once jumped the Pardubice Taxis for a bet, and on another occasion had a race over the steeplechase course the day after the event. He finally called off his 'unofficial entry' when his hunter dumped him at the Log Pile. But fences were much smaller then, and the organization perhaps less formal. Only once did Frank Weldon allow someone to test one of his fences. In 1974 he put a roof over the Whitbread Bar. Master was not convinced that riders would be able to jump the bar without knocking their heads on the crossbars, so his huntsman, Brian Gupwell, jumped through on his hunter, and proved that there were feet to spare. But in general it is a pointless exercise, even though the FEI rules state that an International standard horse must be available to try out the fences if required. Weldon dismisses the idea as a waste of time. 'In no country in the world,' he says logically, 'are you going to have spare horses of that standard who aren't going in for the competition in the first place. And what sort of horse are you going to get to jump over fences of that size in cold blood? It's crazy. As a course builder you have to have the confidence to say to yourself yep, that's right – and stick by it.'

Anyone who, like Frank Weldon, goes on year after year, amazing the spectators and competitors with his originality and ingenuity, becomes almost a slave to his own success. Because people always expect something new and exciting, he feels honour bound to provide it. So far Weldon has never let them down, and he is still bursting with new ideas to incorporate in the cross-country course. His main restriction is the Park itself. When designing the layout and position of fences he has to think of grouping them to accommodate the television coverage. And while the spectators have demonstrated in their thousands that most of them are happy to walk the whole four miles of the cross-country course to see the fences, it is not possible to give them access to every section of the park. As he says, 'Cutting a way through the various woods and fields for the horses is no problem. The real difficulty comes when you have to make gaps four times as wide for the thousands of spectators. It's impossible. It means I've been working with the same blades of grass for the past twenty years. So instead of changing the basic route, if I want to make the whole thing more exciting for the spectators then I have to think of things that are going to titillate their imagination.'

To help give spectators a more educated view of the problems he was setting the riders and the qualities of horsemanship required to tackle them, in 1978 Weldon wrote the first of his programme notes on the psychology behind the course. They are still a regular feature of the programme, and for those who care to read them they offer not only a very valuable insight to the course but also expose a small but revealing aspect of Weldon's vast reservoir of knowledge as both a rider and a course designer. Despite all his responsibilities to satisfy television, ever growing numbers of spectators, and the low key though persistent demands of sponsors, Weldon's first, overriding priority is to go on creating a course that is both the true test of a worthy champion, and an arena in which to hone the talents and abilities of the finest event riders in the world. It is his single-minded dedication to this goal that has made Badminton, as Mark Phillips says, 'Quite simply the biggest and best in the world.'

Behind the scenes during course construction. Top right shows Charlie Chappell, who planted many of the trees now being cut for the Championship fences.

4

THE DIRECTOR

'**I**f Frank Weldon hadn't been forced to spend most of the war in a German prison camp, he'd have left the army a general.' So says His Grace the Duke of Beaufort, David Somerset, President of the Badminton Horse Trials Committee and long-time friend and colleague of Weldon. The Duke's assessment reflects the admiration felt by colleagues and competitors for Weldon's extraordinary powers of leadership and organization.

True, he never made it to general, he retired from the army in 1962 as a lieutenant-colonel. But as far as many people are concerned Frank Weldon has risen way above the rank of general in his civilian job as director of the Badminton Horse Trials (the Whitbread Championship). While the late Duke of Beaufort and his cronies may well have had the foresight and patriotic spirit to establish the event in the first place, it was undoubtedly Weldon's genius as a course builder and 'no nonsense' administrator that salvaged it from decline to make it the most prestigious international event of its kind. Weldon's reputation is enhanced by the fact that he is not just another talented desk-wallah but a horseman of outstanding calibre and reputation, who won every major international equestrian honour of his day, including the Badminton three-day event.

Weldon was a rarity among international riders in the 1950s in that he was entirely 'self made', having never been involved in the specialized, highly concentrated team training that went on with those riders who were already established Olympic hopefuls at the start of the decade. He had ridden ponies as a child in Bombay, and hunted regularly with the Taunton Vale after his family returned to Britain. He admits joining the Army 'only so that I could get into a cavalry regiment and keep riding. But as soon as I joined up they mechanized everything and took the horses away', which wasn't as drastic as it sounds, because eventually he was posted to an artillery unit at Catterick where he had two official Army chargers. 'And you could keep as many other horses as you liked, for just 15 shillings (75p) a week, to cover their insurance.' So Weldon took advantage of the

Colonel Frank Weldon on Kilbarry in 1953 on the final day of Harewood three day event.

Army's generosity, found himself a horse with a fair turn of speed, and concentrated on his main love, steeplechasing; competing, with considerable success, at meetings all over the country. He worked out his own fitness programmes and absorbed details about horses' jumping ability and nimble athleticism that were to prove invaluable once he turned to eventing, and eventually to course building.

In the late 1930s the word eventing did not exist, so there was no way that Weldon could begin to know what an important part it was to play in his life.

Weldon's war was not a glorious one. He spent five years in German prison camps, three of them in Colditz, after several escape attempts in the first two years had labelled him a 'difficult' prisoner. Once back in Britain he picked up the threads of his career, and in 1949 was given the one job he really wanted in the Army – command of the King's Troop at St John's Wood barracks in central London. Racing was still his passion, and winning the Gunners Gold Cup, a race at Sandown just for artillery gunner officers, was his overriding ambition. The young officers at St John's Wood spent their winter weekends hunting, and in the summer dabbled in show jumping. Racing was out of the question, as few – unlike their commanding officer – could afford to buy their own horses. Weldon did not really rate show jumping, and as he recalls: 'Whenever we went to a show a young man called Alan Oliver would turn up with three horses, take first, second and third prize, and leave the scraps for the rest.' So he started looking around for something else that would give his young officers the challenge of competition and possibility of winning. That was when an old general came to dinner in the spring of 1951 and announced that 'you boys ought to be entering for Badminton'. Weldon has often been quoted as saying that as far as he was concerned Badminton was something you played over a net with a bat and a bunch of chicken feathers. But his ears pricked up as the old man went on to describe a competition that included the elements of show jumping, a steeplechase and a ride across country. He was not too sure about 'this thing called dressage', but his appetite had been whetted. The following morning Lieutenant Christopher Morgan was sent off to the BHS headquarters in London's Sloane Square to get more details, and was told to come back just before Christmas for a schedule. When it finally arrived Weldon's reaction was 'Come on boys – let's have a go at this one', and in January, along with four of the officers, he threw himself enthusiastically into preparing for the competition to be staged in April 1952. Weldon admits that he was really only 'going through the motions, because I've always found it easier to lead from the front and say "Follow me", rather than stand back and say "You go and do it".' They did their canter work on the open ground beside Wormwood Scrubs prison, got the horses fit, and fast, by entering race meetings, like the one held by the Pegasus Club for City lawyers, and took their first, faltering steps at dressage in the barracks manège under the expert eye of Jim Russell, who had been an instructor at the old cavalry school at Weedon. Three of the original five riders made it to Badminton, Chris Morgan and John Cameron-Hayes riding their Government chargers Heavy Weather and Water Gypsy, while Weldon took his own grey mare Liza Mandy, who 'jumped like hell out hunting' but did not take kindly to Badminton and dumped her rider at one of the early fences. So while Morgan and Cameron-Hayes finished twelfth and fifteenth respectively, Weldon spent three days in the local cottage hospital with a cracked bone in his neck. As he says, it was 'bad for the image for the lads to do well and the Major to be incapacitated', and it made him more determined than ever to compete successfully the following year. His ambitions were realized through a horse called Kilbarry. Bought in 1952 for £750 from a Midlands farmer, Kilbarry stood at an impressive 17 hands, and though he had never jumped in his life, he was, to Weldon's eye, 'a remarkable horse, absolutely topping', and clearly a mount that could win the Gunners Cup for him.

He won his first point-to-point easily, but then went down with equine flu, and had to be hobdayed to solve respiratory problems, an operation that put a stop to his racing career. However, he was still fast enough for eventing, and although, as Weldon says, 'He made such a hell of a roaring noise through his windpipe you could hear him coming half a mile away, I said, "Kilbarry my boy, you're the chap for me",' and so began a remarkable partnership that was to dominate international eventing for almost five years. Incidentally, Weldon did eventually win the Gunners Gold Cup, on a horse he later bought and trained called Snowshill Lad.

Kilbarry won his very first one-day event, at Stowell Park in spring 1953 as part of his preparation for that year's Badminton competition, which was also the European Championships. The day he arrived in the Badminton stableyard Weldon was asked to become a member of the British team, joining Bertie Hill on Bambi and Reg Hindley on Speculation, and replacing Laurence Rook, whose horse Starlight had a tendency to be highly volatile during the dressage.

Considering that the horse had never completed a three-day event in its life, and

Colonel Frank Weldon and Kilbarry.

its rider had gone round only half of one, it was a risky decision for the selectors to make. But the horse clearly had star quality, and proved it by helping Britain's eventers win their first ever European gold medal, finishing second overall out of forty competitors. Ironically, the competition and individual gold medal was won by Major Rook after Starlight had performed an impeccable dressage test and then stormed across country at a blistering pace. But Weldon's card was marked. He and Kilbarry had joined that small, elite band of horses and riders who went on to fill the record books with their exploits in what are still referred to as Britain's golden years of eventing.

In spring 1954 Tony Collings, who had been the main architect of Britain's training programme from his equestrian centre at Porlock in North Devon, was killed in the first Comet crash on his way to judge a horse show in South Africa. The British team was suddenly without its helmsman, and without hesitation the selection committee approached Weldon, who had already been co-opted onto the newly formed Combined Training Committee the previous year, to become captain of the British three-day event team. It meant that he would be responsible for the training and administration of the team for the European Championships, to be held later that year in Basle and again the following year in Windsor, and for the 1956 Olympics in Stockholm. But first, there was Badminton to concentrate his mind, and for the second year in succession he was runner up, losing to Margaret Hough on Bambi by just 1.6 points. His defeat was made the more bitter by the fact that there were major faults in timekeeping on the steeplechase course, which undoubtedly affected his final score.

While Kilbarry rested, Weldon applied the brisk professionalism that is the hallmark of everything he does to the business of organizing the training of the

British team in co-operation with the Combined Training Committee. He first asked Her Majesty The Queen if they could use the Royal Mews at Windsor Castle, which gave them access to the vast open acreage of Windsor Park, as a training base. A month before flying to Basle (they were one of the first British teams to go by air rather than sea and rail) Diana Mason, Bertie Hill, Laurence Rook and Weldon with their horses Tramella, Crispin, Starlight and Kilbarry went to Windsor to work with former show jumping champion Jack Talbot-Ponsonby and dressage trainer Robert Hall, with Weldon himself applying his racehorse training to getting the horses fit. It paid off. Britain won the gold medal, with Bertie Hill returning in triumph as individual champion. That title passed the following year to Weldon and Kilbarry, when the Championships and the Badminton event were 'moved' to Windsor. One of the main contributions to Britain's success at this time was the emphasis Weldon put on dressage training. British horses were (and still are, he believes) the finest in the world across country, but in the beginning their dressage was simply not good enough. And although Weldon never did enjoy the 'circuits and bumps' of dressage, the hours of concentration and effort began to pay off as British riders repeatedly took top honours. With the Olympic Games in 1956 an obvious goal, Weldon was given a golden opportunity by the Army to prepare for the competition twelve months in advance. His term of command at the King's Troop came to an end in 1955, and as there was almost a year to wait before taking over his next command he took a sabbatical, and spent the entire year racing and preparing Kilbarry for the Olympics. The horse was not beaten in a single competition that autumn or the following spring, so no one was really surprised when he carried off the first prize at Badminton as well. He had, however, been given a run for his money by a young girl called Sheila Willcox, riding in her first Badminton on High and Mighty, who finished the three days just 1.56 points behind him.

The Olympics were held early that year, in May, hard on the heels of Badminton, and there were several raised eyebrows when Weldon decided that the possible Olympic horses should run at Badminton as well, giving them two severe tests in a relatively short space of time. But team captain Weldon was adamant. 'Badminton had to be an Olympic trial. We only had two sure horses, Kilbarry and Countryman, who belonged to the Queen by then but was loaned back to Bertie Hill to ride. We needed a third horse, and the only way to find one was to go for the money and see who came closest.' Despite their obvious brilliance, Sheila Willcox and High and Mighty could not be considered as a partnership as in 1956 women were still not allowed to represent their country in Olympic equestrian sports. Instead, the horse that caught the selectors' eye was Wild Venture, owned by Ted Marsh, who kindly lent him to the team for Laurence Rook to ride. It meant that Britain could send a formidable team to Sweden – three of the most outstanding horsemen in the world, paired with a trio of the finest horses the sport has known; a brilliant combination, which Dorian Williams described as the sort of thing that happens to a nation 'only once in a lifetime'.

Weather conditions for cross-country day in Stockholm were atrocious, and all three riders made a mistake at the same fence, a trakehner in a ditch. That apart, they were unbeatable, and took the team gold, with Weldon and Kilbarry winning the individual bronze medal. For them it had been a spectacular success story. In just four years the Colonel and his 'remarkable horse' had won seven major honours as Badminton, European and Olympic champions. Kilbarry was just ten yeas old, and still in his prime, but his Olympic honour was his last. Early in 1957 he fell at an insignificant fence at the Cottesbroke one-day event, broke his neck, and was killed instantly.

Weldon was shattered. He had adored the horse, and knew he would never find his equal. It was two years before he made any impression again in the eventing world, when in 1959 he finished fifth at Badminton riding Mrs N. Marshall's Samuel Johnson before going on to be runner up in the European Championships at Harewood. His own horse, Fermoy, was nineth at Badminton – Kilbarry was going to be a tough act to follow!

Meanwhile, Weldon had joined the Badminton Committee. Not an onerous job, just one or two meetings a year to discuss general arrangements for the next competition. As he now had a home in Gloucestershire he was also a regular trainer of the Beaufort Hunt Pony Club, where his influence was felt by a group of youngsters who went on to rank among Britain's finest equestrian talents. His 'class of '58', for instance, included Jennie Bullen, now Jennie Loriston-Clarke, one of our finest dressage riders; her sister Jane (now Holderness-Roddam), who won Badminton in 1968 and rode in the gold medal winning Olympic team the same year; Mike Tucker, an international rider and now BBC commentator, and Mark Phillips, Olympic and European gold medalist, and still the only man to have won Badminton four times. In addition, immediately after the Olympic Games Weldon and a German, Count Leopold Rothkirch, plus a Swede, Colonel Gustav Nyblaë, were appointed to produce a set of rules for the three-day event, which until then had apparently survived on a wing and a prayer and the minimum amount of interference from the sport's ruling body, the FEI.

It took them seven months to draw up the first complete set of rules on international three-day events, and Weldon points, with some pride, to the fact that one of the original rules, article 334, has remained unchanged in all those years. It is the rule relating to the time limits for each phase of the speed and endurance, stating clearly how each timed section is quite independent of the rest, and that time saved or lost on one section cannot be added to or taken off another. It is one of the most complicated rules in the book – which is probably why no one has ever tried to tamper with it, though the original is so clearly defined it would be difficult to better.

Kilbarry's death was a watershed for Weldon. He continued to ride, not just his own horse Fermoy but also Samuel Johnson, who again finished in the frame at Badminton in 1960, and Neil Gardiner's Young Pretender, who was second to Anneli Drummond-Hay's Merely-a-Monarch in 1962. But there were years when he did not ride at all. As he says, 'It's not like now, when so many riders have a whole string of horses supplied by a sponsor. We had just one horse. You looked after it, and nursed it to get it to competitions. If you lost that horse for some reason, then you were out, and it took a while to work your way back in.' So in 1962, his fiftieth year, he retired, both from the Army and competitive riding. He reminded me: 'I had ridden in my first Badminton when I was forty, and was forty-three at my first Olympic Games – these days people think you're too old when you're thirty-nine, and I hadn't even started competing then.'

He retained his links with the British team, remaining chef d'équipe until the disastrous Tokyo Olympics of 1964, when Britain was eliminated. In the meantime

Colonel Frank Weldon (left) in 1954 over the Tree Trunk in his stride; with the Duke of Beaufort (right and below right); and with the Duke and Major Laurence Rook in 1985.

he wrote a regular equestrian column for the *Sunday Telegraph*, and ran a small training yard from his home, breaking four-year-olds and schooling horses for a new generation of aspiring event riders. The major turning point came in 1965 when David Somerset, the Duke of Beaufort's heir, became director of Badminton Horse Trials, and asked Frank to join him as course builder. He accepted, and repeated the exercise in 1966, when the event was cancelled because of the appalling weather. But that summer David Somerset played his ace. He invited Weldon to become director of the trials – and he accepted. He says: 'Until then I had never felt tired in my life. I was riding two horses before breakfast, getting into the office at 9 a.m., home again at 5 p.m. to do more work with the horses. But then my girl groom upped and married the best-looking man in the county, and it would have meant starting all over again with someone new in the yard. So I gave up the business with the horses, and concentrated on this job, just about full time.' The result of that full time commitment is now history. In no time at all he had totally reorganized the administration of the event, and was bringing a new excitement and challenge to the course.

For twenty-one years now (and I am writing this in 1986) Frank Weldon has been the most durable, most familiar sight at Badminton – his battered trilby hat shading eyes that miss nothing, and the jaw, set with an ironic grin or clenched in fury, depending on the circumstances of the moment. Weldon admits that he does not suffer fools lightly, and when he barks out a command, in a voice that has been honed razor sharp on young squaddies' livers, he expects to be obeyed. He is one of the 'old school', out of a mould that produced men who demand loyalty and obedience, in return for which they give firm, positive leadership. But Weldon's bark is definitely worse than his bite. And that's his secret. Gruff and terse he might be; but you will not find anyone who has ever been involved with him, competitively or administratively, who does not hold him in the highest esteem, and regard him with great affection. It is true that he and Master, the old Duke of Beaufort, did not always see eye to eye, but they respected each other enormously. The regard showed itself in rather unusual circumstances in 1973. That year there were a number of big drop fences on the course, and as Weldon tells it, 'From a

public point of view, if riders don't get round it's because Weldon's been beastly to them, and that year there was a lot of bellyaching afterwards.' Certainly, some of the concern on this occasion came from Her Majesty The Queen, who had been watching Princess Anne compete on Goodwill. The combination finished fourth, but with the natural concern of a mother the Queen voiced her feelings to Master, who later told Weldon he thought the course had been 'rather unfair'. Weldon was stung by the remarks, so much so that both David Somerset and Laurence Rook were convinced that he was going to resign. Some weeks later, on the way back from a fishing trip to Scotland, the Duke delivered the biggest salmon he had caught to Weldon's back door as a peace offering, and the troubled waters were smoothed.

Weldon's courses are certainly never easy, and they are not intended to be. The combination of obstacles remains one of the most formidable equestrian tests in the world, so it is perhaps proof of the genuine equality of eventing, as one of the rare sporting challenges where men and women really do compete on equal terms, that since Weldon took over as course builder in 1965 the event has been won on ten occasions by a man, and also on ten occasions by a woman rider, with Lucinda Green claiming the title a record-breaking six times. At world, European and Olympic competitions women riders have been proving their great skill and courage, from the outstanding success of Sheila Willcox in the late 1950s to the golden run of Virginia Holgate (now Leng) in the mid 1980s. In spite of this Weldon is unrepentantly chauvinistic. 'If I had any choice, I'd much rather have four men in a team than girls,' he says. 'You get a stiff, tough course, and the man, if he's any good, just sticks his jaw out, says a rude word, and gets on with it. The girls, they may be as brave, sometimes even braver, more gutsy than the men. But what distresses me is that you see a little tear appear in the corner of her eye, and she sniffs. It's because they have a different mental approach to the thing. They're very good, and there's no doubt about it, but I'd still rather have four Mark Todds than four Virginia Holgates.' Then he adds, with a wink and a grin, as if to soften the blow, 'Mind you, I'd rather look at the girls any day.' And if that doesn't earn him the title MCP of the Year from Britain's ladies, nothing will. But then Weldon is a man who is not afraid to speak his mind, and claims the privilege of age to be allowed his opinions.

In 1987 the director of Badminton Horse Trials will be seventy-four years old – nine years past the age of retirement. Friends and colleagues may ask anxiously, 'How much longer can he go on, and what will happen when he leaves?' But Weldon marches to his own drum, and he is clearly not yet ready to hand over the reins. 'I have thought about it,' he admits, 'and it's been nagging on my conscience. But it's no good suggesting that I take on someone to train for the job, because I'm not the sort of person who can have someone tagging along saying "What are you going to do next?" every five minutes.' It is true that the whole Badminton operation is run on the lines of a benevolent dictatorship – even Weldon himself did not disagree with that description when I put it to him. And because he recognizes the strength of his own personality, he is the first to admit that whoever takes over from him eventually will want that same degree of authority. He says candidly, 'They won't want the old fool [referring to himself] telling them what they should have done. It's ridiculous. They'll have to find out for themselves, and do things their own way.'

It is a practical and generous man who recognizes that, as he himself made sweeping changes when he took over more than twenty years ago, so his successor might want to follow suit, and make his, or her, own stamp on the event. I suspect he knows exactly what he would like to see happen when he retires – the establishment of a joint directorship, with one person designing the course, another responsible for the administration. I even suspect that he knows precisely who he would like to see fill the two posts. But one thing is certain: like his old partner Kilbarry, whatever happens Weldon is going to be a tough act to follow.

5

MONEY MATTERS

If the Badminton three-day event had originally been conceived as a commercial venture and not a sporting one, it would probably never have survived past 1966. This is a sobering thought for an event that now has a turnover of something well in excess of £½ million a year. Not to put too fine a point on it, in the mid 1960s the sport of eventing was in such an appalling state, commercially and competitively, that the whole lot, not just the Badminton event, was about to get the chop.

The British three-day event teams had won nothing internationally since the European Championships in 1957, and had been humiliated at two Olympic Games. From the BHS headquarters in London came ominous rumblings suggesting that in view of this abysmal record the entire horse trials division should be scrapped. It was an argument fuelled by the fact that attendances at Badminton were falling, and as the Society was then responsible for staging the event it had to bear huge financial losses for three years, offset only by meagre profits of about £3000 in the good years. Even the sport's first champion, the Duke of Beaufort, was having his doubts, declaring to close associates, 'All we seem to be getting is more of these round-bottomed girls, who aren't any good anyway, and we always get beat. I don't know why we bother to go on doing this.' The Duke never could come to terms with the excellence of Britain's women riders, but considering his impact on the sport as a whole perhaps he should be allowed that one little foible! What is much more important is that here was the man who had effectively started the sport in this country actually considering withdrawing his patronage because he no longer felt it was worth while. For a few months the future of Badminton really was in jeopardy.

Fortunately, Frank Weldon had other ideas. He admits that he is no financier, though he adds with one of those characteristic winks, 'but I'm no fool either, and I flatter myself that I know how many beans make five as well as most people,' which to those who know this wily old campaigner is something of an understatement – to put it mildly. While the BHS was flapping and talking cancellation, Weldon could see the enormous commercial potential of the event, provided that it was run efficiently. He is uncompromising in his attitude to the state of affairs at that time: 'It was,' he says, 'the most inefficiently run thing you can imagine.' So in 1966, when David Somerset asked him to become not just the course builder and his assistant, as he had been for the previous two competitions, but the director, Weldon agreed on the understanding that he and not the BHS would be responsible for the whole shebang, including the accounts. And knowing Frank Weldon, I can well imagine the anticipatory gleam that came into his eye when David Somerset agreed.

His goal was quite simple. 'I had to make it viable'. That meant attacking the sporting and commercial problems simultaneously. Increasing the severity of the fences and making Badminton the most respected course in the world was central to his whole strategy. Comparing his tactics with those used in the theatre, he was wise enough to observe, 'It doesn't matter how brilliant your box office, your organization, advertising and everything else is, the product has got to be right. If it's not, you simply won't get the audience. And there's no shadow of doubt in my mind that what people come here for is to watch the boys and girls risking their necks on the cross-country.'

So while the course builders were constructing some of those early innovative Weldon fences, he was performing equally revolutionary changes to Badminton's commercial attitudes. The first job was to put everything under one roof in the Badminton Horse Trials office, in the building they still occupy in the main street opposite the Post Office. Before that Gordon Cox-Cox had worked out of a room above the Badminton Estate Office, while the BHS ran the organization from its offices in London. A few advance tickets, perhaps sixty or seventy but surprisingly no more, were sold, and then a mobile office was set up in a caravan in Portcullis Yard, behind Badminton House, two weeks before the competition started. Trade stand exhibitors were organized by a firm from Gravesend in Kent, who gave the BHS just 10 per cent of the proceeds. Weldon recognized immediately that this was one area in which Badminton could start showing a profit. Regular exhibitors must have been a bit shocked when they received their annual letter, not, as before, pointing out in somewhat genteel terms that as they had supported Badminton in the past perhaps they would like to come again, but Weldon's more businesslike version, which effectively said, 'This is a most prestigious event . . . you have the opportunity to come if you want, but if not, say so now because there are plenty who do.' As he says, 'It worked like a charm'. In spite of an increase in ground rent, exhibitors were clamouring to get space at the event, and by the end of 1968 the accounts were healthily in the black, where they have stayed ever since.

The recovery was remarkable, and with some pride Weldon can plot the increase in attendance at a steady 20 per cent a year, until the numbers finally levelled off in 1980. Even so, there is still a steady 4 to 5 per cent increase in the number of spectators, especially on Thursday and Friday, when many of the 'old hands' come to watch some of the dressage, get their shopping done from the trade stands without too much of a crush, then go off to walk the cross-country course before returning home to watch the entire thing on television. However you look at it, Badminton is now an impressive financial enterprise. It costs over £350,000 to stage, and still turns in a satisfyingly substantial profit each year.

*Above: Virginia Leng (née Holgate) with
autograph hunters, 1985.
Right: Virginia Leng on Priceless, 1985.*

Considering the size of the operation, it is a relatively inexpensive thing to stage, mainly because, as Weldon says, he gets 'as many people as possible to do as much as possible for nothing'. That may sound mercenary, but it is based on a long tradition of generous help from the Beaufort Hunt, Badminton villagers, and every 'neighbour' in the vicinity, who have given their help as stewards, fence judges, timekeepers, vets, medical staff and so on since the very first year in 1949. Their 'reward' is a personal invitation from the Duke to a cocktail party in Badminton House on the Thursday of Championship week. To an outsider that may sound rather feudal... but there is nothing condescending about the gesture or the evening. Master instigated the practice, and the present Duke is happy to continue what is a genuine expression of thanks for the generosity of the community. Without that huge willing reservoir of free labour Badminton would be almost prohibitively expensive. As it is, all costs are kept to a minimum. The only salaries are paid to the small permanent staff of treasurer and assistant director, Major Derek Dyson, the event secretary, Jane Gundry, and her assistant, Sue Ingall, to Jill Brookes who runs the box office, and of course Frank Weldon himself, who drew just £300 in expenses during his first year, before putting the whole thing on a more businesslike footing.

The rest of that £350,000 is taken up with the running expenses that make the event operable – like paying for the labour and machinery actually to build the course each year, erecting the grandstand, laying temporary tracking for roads, meeting the printer's bill for thousands of programmes, car stickers, official badges and grandstand tickets, erecting dozens of temporary toilets, providing a public address system, paying for the accommodation of foreign competitors and the official ground jury, buying the rosettes, paying for the car park attendants and official litter collectors, and paying the considerable premium on the insurance that protects their investment should the event have to be cancelled. Derek Dyson's shopping list is the very framework of the organization, and he knows that once they have paid all the bills the first thing to come out of the profits is their donation to the BHS. Since taking over the running of the event, Badminton has made an annual donation to the Society to help fund the Horse Trials Section. Like everything else, that figure has increased with the sport's popularity, soaring from an initial £6000 paid in 1969 to the present figure of £90,000. The rest of the profit is ploughed back into the Badminton estate and the event itself, paying for Weldon's drainage and land improvement schemes, as well as compensating the Duke for the use of his 'front garden'. For as Weldon says, 'Longleat has its lions, Beaulieu has its cars, and we just have horses four days in the year', so the trick is to make the maximum profit in the minimum amount of time.

And it is the great British public who flock to the event in their thousands who guarantee the event's financial success. Over four days a third of a million people make the annual pilgrimage, with at least 200,000 turning up solely for cross-country day. On average, one in four of them will buy the glossy competition programme, selling in 1986 at £1.50; their cars cost anything from £6 to £13 to park, depending on which day they attend; seats in the 6000-seater grandstand range from £2.50 to £7.50 for the dressage and show jumping. That all adds up to a considerable sum, but it is not just the money they pay to get in that makes the balance sheet look so healthy, it is the fact that they represent a third of a million prospective customers to the trade stands. The promise of that captive audience guarantees a solid core of regular exhibitors prepared to pay the ever-increasing fees that are the bedrock of Badminton's financial success.

Badminton's Bond Street, as it has always been known, has grown from a handful of hopefuls in 1949 to a veritable tented hypermarket, which had 265 'shops' in 1986 providing all the goods and services you would expect to find in any major provincial shopping centre. This substantial commercial empire is the domain of Badminton's assistant director Derek Dyson, who had ridden the course in the mid 1950s and joined brother-in-law Frank Weldon in 1970, just at the point when Badminton was beginning to become a major commercial venture. There were fewer than eighty exhibitors when he joined the team, all neatly arranged in a single avenue to one side of the grandstand. Over the years he has taken up more and more ground, as the single avenue first stretched closer to the house, then became two avenues, and now needs a third site, on Park Piece close to the car park, to accommodate those who see Badminton in commercial terms as a major financial opportunity. As a result, above the smell of horses the pervading odour is one of profit, and the atmosphere that of a mutually beneficial partnership.

It costs anything from £130 to £700 just to book the ground for those exhibitors who want to bring in their own caravans or mobile exhibition trailers, while the hire of one of the ready-made canvas 'shops' can cost anything from £265 for the smallest to £865 for a 30-foot frontage, with flooring, trestle tables, chairs and electricity all going down on the bill as extras. Once they have achieved a foothold in Badminton Bond Street, very few exhibitors ever leave. Every year there is a long waiting list of at least fifty hopefuls, of whom perhaps two or three might be accepted, and even then it means being given a site in Park Piece, slightly out on a limb from the rest of the trade stands, with the hope of graduating to the main avenue when one of the regulars drops out. Clearly Bond Street is the place to be. On all four days, regardless of the drama and excitement taking place out on the cross-country course or in the main arena, the shopping avenue is always thick with people buying everything from beer and hot dogs to a new car, a complete set of clothes or an original oil painting. Derek Dyson admits that he stopped being amazed years ago by the people who want to exhibit at the show. 'We have to try and limit the number of saddlers who come,' he says, 'otherwise at an event like this we'd be overrun with them. But apart from that really anyone with anything to sell wants to come here.' And he cites the example of a newcomer, who arrived early in the 1970s, and turned out to be a toy shop. He admits, 'I thought we'd made a terrible mistake, but then at the end of the competition the owner came to us and proudly showed a selection of photographs in which nearly every member of the Royal family had visited his stand to buy toys. He was practically "By Appointment", and he came regularly after that until a few years ago when he retired.'

Dyson admits that as far as commercial space is concerned they have reached saturation point. Although companies are still clamouring to be given space, there is simply nowhere else for them to go. Casual observers have suggested that perhaps the stands could extend further into the car park area from Park Piece, but with commendable honesty Dyson admits, 'It really would be counterproductive. It's miles from the main action of the day, and I don't think anyone would really find it very worthwhile to go there.'

In 1986 there was an unexpected bonus. Frank Weldon was able to move the start of the course a little nearer the house, and made room for another twenty trade stands. Simultaneously, as a result of the Bradford fire disaster, the fire department insisted that they leave gaps between some of the stands as a fire break, so the extra sites were reduced to twelve. 'But that really is it,' says Dyson, 'and frankly it's a good job we did find that extra ground, because with the new regulations we were reaching the stage where we might have had to chuck someone out.'

In contrast, the business in hospitality marquees is still expanding – those super-sized tents bedecked with flowers, draped with gauze and ribbons, lit by expensive chandeliers, where major national and international companies can wine and dine with their clients amid the atmosphere of a unique country spectacle. The first six arrived on the scene in 1979. Six years later there were sixteen of them, with the largest paying almost £1700 each for their sites. Their concentration in the vicinity of the main arena is not as critical as for the trade stands, so clearly this is one area of business still ripe for development.

Television is another source of income. The BBC paid £21,000 in 1986 to screen Badminton highlights over three days on both channels. An even larger slice of Badminton's revenue comes from its sponsors, Whitbread. They now pay in excess of £120,000 for the privilege of associating themselves commercially with the greatest event of its kind in the world. Frank Weldon states candidly, 'We could manage very well without sponsorship. It's just a fraction of our turnover ... though it does help to bump up the profit.' This might explain the somewhat cautious statement from Whitbreads marketing manager, Tim O'Neill, that sponsor and client have what is 'not always a happy relationship, more a stable affair in which both partners are reasonably happy bedfellows'.

The Whitbread association began in 1961, more as a friendly gesture on the part of Colonel Bill Whitbread to his close friend and neighbour the Duke of Beaufort than as a commercial venture. In its first year Badminton had offered a prize of £150 to the owner of the winning horse. In 1950 the *Daily Telegraph* stepped in and offered a cup for the winner, but the prize money was still coming out of the BHS budget, and this remained unchanged until 1960.

It is said that the suggestion of sponsorship was made at a dinner party in Badminton House, when Master casually mentioned to Colonel Whitbread that it was something he might like to consider to give the sport a bit of a boost. By then Whitbreads were already associated with horses and sponsorship through the racing world, so eventing was just a sideways step in the same direction. Colonel Whitbread agreed, and through his generosity the prize money in 1961 totalled 1600 sovereigns. The first prize shot up to £250, and the famous Whitbread Trophy made its first appearance. Over the years the money has gradually increased, and while it has never been in the same league as that paid in racing or show jumping, Badminton has remained the richest prize in the eventing calendar at £6,000 to the winner. When you consider that keeping a three-day event standard horse on the circuit, with all the travelling, training and competition fees, plus food, stabling, vet and blacksmith bills can cost around £10,000 a year according to three of the major sponsors, it's obvious that event riders are not in the sport for the money.

Above: Nigel Taylor on Full Swing at the roads and tracks, 1986.
Right: Lucinda Green receiving the Whitbread Trophy for the fifth time from Her Majesty The Queen, 1983.
Below: It's thirsty work watching others ride so skilfully.

In addition to increased prize money, the sponsorship has also meant that Badminton can offer free stabling, bedding and forage to its competitors, and is still the only competition of its kind in the world that gives free accommodation and food to all grooms. In return for this financial support, for years Whitbread seem to have got very little out of the deal. There were no official contracts. The whole thing was, according to Frank Weldon, a gentleman's agreement with Colonel Bill never wanting to exploit the situation or his friendship with the Duke and make overt commercial capital out of his association with the event. A quaintly paternalistic attitude, compared to today's thrusting commercial approach, but one that Colonel Bill and his company were happy to go along with. They had a small hospitality tent, and an office from which the winner could collect his or her trophies, and there were one or two Whitbread advertisements around the place, but that was all. It was Frank Weldon's own suggestion that he should build the now famous Whitbread Bar as the last fence in 1966 – the year after he took over. Twelve years later the Whitbread Drays made their first appearance. But it was 1980 before the words 'For the Whitbread Trophy' were added on the front cover of the official programme, in small letters under the name 'Badminton Horse Trials', and that same year the Whitbread Beer Barrels were given their prominent position as the first fence on the cross-country course.

There was clearly a very warm and comfortable relationship between those concerned, if not a particularly hard-nosed commercial one. But in July 1984 all that changed. Colonel Bill and a number of senior board members retired, to be replaced by a new generation who saw the large sums of money being handed over every year as something more than just patronage. In fact these were large enough for someone to question why it was being done. Tim O'Neill was brought in, with a budget and a brief, to make Badminton commercially worthwhile to Whitbread. 'We couldn't go on saying "Let's do this because it's a hobby of the Chairman's",' he says. 'There was just too much money involved. We had to justify that expenditure.' 1985 was very much a 'getting to know you' period for the new Whitbread management and the old Badminton Committee. That year the sponsors handed over £82,500, and when the competition was over Tim O'Neill began negotiating a three-year contract on the principal that it would take at least that long for any new investment to show a benefit.

Return on investment is the name of the game, and O'Neill admits that if he couldn't justify the huge sums of money being paid out each year, it was unlikely that Whitbread would have wanted the partnership to continue. 'It has to deliver a quantifiable commercial return,' is how he puts it, and says, 'There are four major reasons for sponsoring an event: to provide an environment in which to entertain our customers and key performers, to promote company values, the company name, and most importantly, our products.'

In fact Badminton satisfied all those criteria and has now become, like any other major sponsored event, a four-day vehicle for a concentrated advertising campaign. Compared with many it is still relatively low key, but spectators in 1986 could not fail to notice the increased Whitbread presence. The event is now officially called the Whitbread Championships, a subtle move that ensures free publicity for the company name every time it is mentioned by the press, radio and television. All the major road signs and hoardings in the vicinity of the competition point you towards and welcome you to the 'Whitbread Championships', and at each fence there are now large boards bearing the company's name as well as the name of the individual fence. It will take years, of course, before people generally stop calling it simply 'Badminton', but for the moment at least the name Whitbread is a prominent feature and certainly fulfils the advertising objectives.

Less obvious to the spectator, but still a vital part of the operation, they now have the franchise on all the beer sold over the four days, and provide an increasing amount of the public catering. They improved facilities for the 300 members of the press corps (a smart piece of press/public relations, as reporters are more likely to be generous to you if they are working in comfortable surroundings) and Whitbread entertained more than a thousand private guests and their families in an enlarged, positively luxurious marquee. For all this Whitbread now pay a sum that is well into six figures, and do so willingly believing that they do now get something in return for that hefty cheque.

Both sides readily admit that the partnership may not continue indefinitely, though without any sponsorship money at all Badminton's profits would drop considerably, and if another company took over from Whitbread they might demand a more high profile image and even greater commercial identification. But for the moment this scenario remains hypothetical, and the partners inhabit a middle ground of compromise in which both appear to be relatively satisfied, and neither feels threatened or compromised. There have, of course, been disagreements and problems. One of the most vociferous was over the new look given to the cover of the official programme. For years the pencil drawings of equine artist Joan Wanklin captured the very essence of Badminton, with a muscular, competitive horse at full stretch over one of the identifiable fences. Whitbread considered the drawings expert, but old-fashioned, and in 1985 introduced a clinical white cover bearing just the name of the championship, with a top hat, a velvet hunting cap and a crash helmet symbolizing the three stages of the competition. Frank Weldon described it as 'a bloody hat shop', and Tim O'Neill agreed it was 'not a very good start'. For the following year a team of highly experienced commercial artists was employed to find a suitable alternative and finally, at the fourth attempt, came up with the present logo – a horse and rider, jumping over a sash bearing the inscription Whitbread Championships, all contained within a cricle containing the one word 'Badminton'. The purists still say the horse looks more like a show jumper than an eventer, but like so many things in the new partnership it is a compromise, and one that O'Neill feels really does put across the new message 'that this isn't just a glorified support Badminton event – this is a major competition backed by professional sponsorship which is professionally run'. There is no question of the increased participation of the sponsors actively changing the character of the sport. Apart from the fact that Weldon would not allow it, even the sharpest financial mind can see that too much commercial 'tinkering' would destroy the very nature of the event, which makes it such a crowd puller in the first place. Because frankly it does not really matter whose name appears over the sponsors' tent, or even if that space remained blank. Badminton may well provide what O'Neill describes as 'numerous commercial opportunities', but essentially this event is all about bold horses and courageous riders jumping over demanding and sometimes terrifying obstacles. While it can maintain that combination the crowds will keep coming in their thousands, and that alone is money in the bank.

AS SEEN ON
TELEVISION

When Badminton first launched itself on a totally inexperienced and unsuspecting public back in 1949, it is unlikely that more than a thousand people made their way to this corner of the Gloucestershire countryside to see what was prophetically described as 'the greatest three-day event in the world'. Now, more than eight million people are annually thrilled and entertained by the spectacle in the comfort of their own homes sitting in front of the television. For as far as the BBC's outside broadcast unit is concerned, the Whitbread Championships at Badminton is one of the major sporting events in the calendar, ranking alongside the Grand National, the Cup Final and Wimbledon.

Over two days they screen more than two and a half hours of live and recorded highlights of the event through the skills of a veritable army of production and technical staff, engineers and commentators. In the main control vehicle the current Badminton producer, Johnny Wotherstone, sits at the centre of a web of electronic gadgetry and facilities that enable him to call up the pictures from thirteen cameras, and transmit them live or recorded, in slow motion or speeded up, with or without a digital clock giving the current running time, with or without a commentary. All the tricks of the television trade are employed to meet the demands and the appetite of a viewing public that has come to expect all the atmosphere and drama of a live sporting event.

There is no doubt that over the years television has made eventing a major spectator sport, taking it to a vast non-horsy set who would never dream of going anywhere near a dressage arena or a cross-country course, and yet for whom riders like Lucinda Green, Ginny Leng and Richard Meade have become household names. Certainly British successes at the Olympic, European and World Championships in the late 1960s and early 1970s made people more aware of the sport, and eager to see it 'in the flesh', as it were. Equally, a great many of the spectators who began swelling the ranks at the event during that time were people who had had their appetite whetted by the television coverage and wanted a close-up view

*David Green away from the footbridge on Mairangi
Bay, 1983.*

without the barrier of the electronic screen, especially after the advent of colour in 1968 which turned the whole thing into a technicolour parade of horses and riders against the lush green parkland of the English countryside. Ironically, it is the quality of the television coverage that now persuades many people to stay away from the event, knowing they can get a better, more comprehensive view from home, something that early television viewers could never claim. According to Jack Belascoe, 'All you could see were riders in black or white shirts going around on things that were black or white lumps with a leg at each corner' – a graphic, if not particularly inspiring, view of coverage in those burgeoning years. Jack Belascoe was head of engineering at BBC Bristol, which had responsibility for staging the original outside broadcasts. He admits he is not much of a horseman, but for a while his impressions were evidently shared by a vast non-riding audience, who needed the advent of colour to attract their attention. Once that happened, as one of the earliest producers, Peter Bale, recalls, 'Suddenly there was this awareness that this was a magnificent sporting occasion coming from the country home of a Duke. It really had a dramatic effect.'

Television coverage started in 1954. That was the year Gordon Cox-Cox took over as director, and the competition advertised itself as being run for the 'Individual Championship of Great Britain and Northern Ireland'. No doubt mindful of the fact that the televison commentators, as well as the public, would like a few more details about the competitors and their horses, the programme for the first time contained the sort of biographical notes on the competitors and their horses that are now a regular feature. These were early days, when the qualifications to enter Badminton were limited to being a member of the BHS and having a horse that was born in or before 1948, so to modern sportsmen the biographies are somewhat bizarre. For instance, among the forty-nine entries we find May Morning, a seven-year-old 16.2 hand brown gelding who had 'hunted hard all season with the Meath Hounds, Ward Union Stag Hounds and Littlegrange Harriers in Ireland'. A Grade A show jumper called Djort, from Chippenham in Wiltshire, was eliminated on cross-country day after three refusals at the Coffin. In contrast Mr H. Freeman-Jackson, the captain of Ireland's 1952 Olympic team, rode Brown Sugar, and was placed fifth, while a charger from the King's Troop called Water Gypsy was listed as having ridden in the Coronation parade the year before. It finished a creditable sixteenth ridden by Major Derek Dyson – who was much later to become second in command to Frank Weldon as deputy director of the event.

The first pictures the television audience saw of Badminton were shown on the Friday evening when a recording of some of the day's dressage was included in the sports section of the evening news. In 1954 there was no telerecording as we know it today. Things were either live or filmed. So the 'live' pictures that were shot during Friday afternoon were transmitted to London, where a film camera was set up in front of a television screen to film the action. All very primitive and Heath Robinson – but it worked. This film was then edited and put out that evening as edited highlights. As Jack Balesco says, 'The quality was atrocious, but that was the only way to set it on the air.' On the Saturday afternoon of 22 April 1954, the nation saw Badminton's cross-country phase televised live for the first time. There were just six cameras covering the event, which meant that the majority of the thirty-five fences were never seen at all. There were two mobile control rooms, through which the producer could monitor the shots coming from the cameras. One unit had been borrowed from the BBC in Birmingham, complete with three cameras, and a spare, and was positioned at Cape Farm, while the second vehicle came from Bristol, again with three cameras and a spare, and was stationed by the lake near the start of the course. Each camera had just 1000 ft of cable, so there was a limit to how far they could go from the central control point. It meant they could get pictures of the lake and the Coffin, and a few of the fences in the vicinity of the Vicarage fields. But what happened in the old Quarry, and the fences through the wooded plantations to the left and rear of Badminton House remained a mystery.

Throughout the Saturday afternoon the unit provided live coverage of the event, between trips to speedway, motor racing and the rest of the weekend's sporting events, much as they do now, with the film camera in London still recording every frame to replay as highlights later in the evening. Dorian Williams was the commentator, installed in the famous Badminton Bus, the command HQ where he could watch the action on a single black and white television monitor, and keep in touch with the scores and fortunes of each rider as they were relayed to the director, Gordon Cox-Cox.

Then, as now, riders began each phase in accordance with a strict timetable, so it was always fairly easy to inform the central control in London when a particularly notable rider was about to set off. Unfortunately, not everyone in London realized the importance of maintaining that strict timetable, and Peter Bale recalls that in

*Above: BBC Outside Producer John
Wotherstone in the TV scanner room, the
nerve centre of the television coverage.
Right: Rachel Hunt and Piglet II at the
Whitbread Drays, 1984.
Below: Beverley Thomas and Divine
Inspiration, 1984.*

Above: Presentation by Her Majesty The Queen to Lucinda Green.
Left and below: The BBC and the tangle of cables behind the scenes.

the early years it was not unusual for a head of sport to bellow down the line from London, 'Why can't you hurry up and get those bloody horses started?'

On the Saturday evening the Birmingham unit packed up their cameras, rolled up the cables, and left for home. The following day they were due to be part of a unit covering a Sunday service. The Bristol cameramen moved their equipment into the show jumping ring, ready to provide live coverage of the closing stages of the competition – the show jumping and prize giving. The scene was set for an exciting finish. Major (as he was then) Frank Weldon and Kilbarry, who had been members of the winning 1953 European Championships team, were in the lead a full 18 points ahead of Margaret Hough on Bambi V, a horse she had loaned for the Olympics in 1952. There were rumblings about an error in the timing on the steeplechase course having robbed Weldon of extra bonus points, but with an 18 point lead he looked a sure fire winner, and even Weldon himself admits that 'in those days we didn't kick up a fuss about things like that'. So the public were ready for a popular win. But then Kilbarry had two fences down, and as there were ten penalties added for every show jumping mistake, twenty penalties meant he dropped to second place, and Badminton had its first lady winner in Margaret Hough. The whole drama, controversy and nail-biting climax had been captured on television, albeit in black and white and with limited technical resources. But Badminton had proved it had viewer appeal, and the pattern was set for what has become an annual sporting highlight.

Throughout the 1950s Dorian Williams established himself as the BBC's man at Badminton. He introduced the programmes, provided all the commentary, did the interviews and gave expert comment, as well as doing the commentary for the public address system on the course. In 1957 he was joined by a new recruit to the eventing world, Raymond Brookes-Ward, who recalls, 'I was just the lad. I did anything nobody else wanted to do on the public address, like announce lost children or whatever. Nothing grand. I did some of the scores on dressage day, a bit of commentary on the cross-country, and then they let me do the show jumping because I'd done a bit for the BBC from the Horse of the Year Show in 1956.' He was also seconded to the BBC radio unit to provide live and recorded highlights for the listeners to the Light Programme and Home Service, though he went to Badminton not really having a clue what it was all about and never having seen the event before – an unthinkable situation for a commentator these days. In mitigation he adds, 'You see, the whole thing was more like a very cosy gymkhana in those days. All terribly homely, more like one of today's one-day events.' And that 'homeliness' was evident right through the organization, particularly in the way the Royal family regarded the event. Peter Bale recalls how on one occasion Lord Snowdon popped his head round the control room door during transmission and asked if it would be all right for him and 'the family' to come in and watch what was going on. Peter naturally said yes, so Lord Snowdon, Princess Margaret and their two children made themselves comfortable at the back of the truck. Eventually young Lady Sarah asked if they could 'find Grandma for me', so one of the cameramen duly located the Queen Mother, sitting on the grass by the Lake fence, chatting unconcernedly with the spectators around her. Hearing Peter Bale tell me that story prompted Jack Belascoe to recall an occasion when the cameras had not been so welcome. When the outside broadcast unit were parked by the lake it meant that they were directly in front of the house. Part of the equipment included a huge aerial needed for transmission. One year the security police at Badminton made the BBC lower the aerial and move it, because they were convinced that the engineers had put a camera on top which could look straight into the Queen's bedoom at the front of Badminton House. They had not of course, but the police were not convinced, and the aerial was moved!

The cosy atmosphere could not and did not last. The expansion within the sport in general, and Badminton in particular, is reflected directly in the scale and development of the BBC's own involvement. 1959 was a major watershed – quite literally. The atrocious weather conditions of bitterly cold wind and seemingly neverending rain, had turned the Park into a quagmire. Seeing the mess caused by the dressage arena and car park right in front of the house, the Duke insisted that the following year the whole thing should be moved to higher ground away from the house. The combination of horses and cars had chewed the ground into a muddy field, but the BBC played its part in the decision too. The huge outside broadcast vehicles were bogged down in the mud alongside the lake, and the only way to get them out was to bring in a pair of massive tractors with caterpillar tracks, and drag the deadweight vehicles out sideways. When they had finished the park looked as though it had been the site of a crazy ploughing match, and the Duke went 'berserk'.

The following year the Beeb was given its now permanent site just behind the site of the main arena, where the enclosure has been underpinned with hardcore to prevent a repeat of the 'ploughing'.

Throughout the 1960s television reaped the benefits of a boom in electronic innovation. It became possible to video record with huge machines in London, and 'play back' material recorded only minutes earlier. Within a few years mobile recorders were developed and fitted into the outside broadcast equipment so that whole packages could be recorded and edited on site, without the delay of having to relay the material to London. A video disc was invented, giving slow motion replay – quite a revolution at the time – which meant that the commentators could analyse every stride into and over a jump. And then came the great breakthrough – colour. As Peter Bale says, 'It really had a huge impact'. From then on it was a question of how sophisticated the system would allow you to be with the coverage. 'I know,' he admits, 'that some of the "old guard" at Badminton were a bit wary of how we would treat the event. With all the razzmatazz of the new technology, there were fears that we would perhaps turn it into something that it never was.' But fortunately by then there were enough people involved with the production who understood the sport, and knew that this was one event you could play straight. There was enough excitement and spectacle in the sight of horse and rider challenging the increasingly demanding fences without looking for excuses to jazz it up visually.

As Jack Belascoe says, 'From our point of view, as engineers, the Badminton story is one of technical innovation', but apart from having a striking impact on the way the event looked on television, the new equipment triggered off another important development. It made it abundantly clear that the whole thing was getting far too big for Bristol to handle. Looking back, Peter Bale says, 'The event started to take us over. Each year we were using more and more cameras which we scrounged from Birmingham, Manchester, London, wherever we could get them. But it soon beame obvious that the event required a huge concentration of sophisticated equipment which we just didn't have.' So in the early 1970s the whole operation was taken over by the BBC's main outside broadcast division in London, who could legitimately call on equipment and personnel from anywhere in the country. At the same time Frank Weldon's appointment as director in 1967 was beginning to take effect. No one in that position before had appreciated the importance of publicity and television coverage in the way that Weldon did. He saw television as the perfect means of taking Badminton to a vast audience and ensuring its success as a commercial enterprise as well as a sporting one. So he discussed his course in advance with the outside broadcast producer, in great detail, explaining exactly where the fences would be and ensuring that the cameras got the best position to give maximum coverage. Over the previous ten years television engineers had developed thinner, more efficient cables so that the cameramen were no longer tied to their limiting 1000 ft umbilical cord, but could move out into the previously inaccessible locations on the course, while developments in the cameras themselves meant that the old 'movietone' models, on which you had actually to change the lens if you wanted to go from a long shot to a close-up, had been replaced by the 'zoom' lens, which could follow a rider in one long, continuous sweep from one fence to another. Badminton had come of age as a television spectacle. The technology enhanced it, and the event's director positively encouraged it.

There was, however, one casualty in the coverage – dressage. According to a former head of sport, Brian Cowgill (who later became controller of BBC 1), watching dressage was about as exciting as 'watching the bloody grass grow'. It had to go. Occasionally you will still get a glimpse of it as part of a compilation of the three days' events shown on BBC2's Sunday afternoon coverage. But essentially the television coverage of Badminton is all about the speed and endurance of day two, and the nail-biting conclusion of day three in the show jumping ring – and that's what you get.

Johnny Wotherstone is quite clear about his responsibility to the viewers. 'It's twofold. First and foremost it's to reflect the drama of the competition of the day, which is the cross-country – obviously the most important phase, and the excitement which is part of that, and then the overall atmosphere of the place. It's weaving those elements together to reflect the event that it is, which is something far greater than being just the horse trials.' As in all successful programming, achieving that end calls for the unbeatable combination of professional competence and meticulous planning. In January he makes the first of a number of visits to the site, just to get the general impression of where the fences will be, how they will look, and where best to place the thirteen cameras available to him. Later, with engineering and production staff there will be more visits, to finalize locations, work out the complexities of laying thousands of feet of cable across the Park to each of the camera stations, and the logistics of getting 110 members of staff and their assorted vehicles and equipment on site and operational.

Positioning the cameras to get maximum coverage and effect is the key, and Wotherstone works to a set formula: 'I always start at the last fence and work backwards'. His reasoning is simple: 'Because we have to think in terms of what it will look like on transmission. When we have a live inject into Grandstand it's better to be able to have one rider on a run in to the finish, especially if it's clear that someone is going to finish in a fast time, then we can make a feature of them from at least half way round. So I start by working that out, and then obviously go for the hardest, most spectacular fences, like the Lake, which is always dramatic, and the Quarry, and Vicarage Vee where anyone who attempts that yawning corner takes a terrific leap.' Looking at replays of previous years it certainly does look very 'spectacular', and proves Wotherstone's point that it's not just where you place the cameras that's important, but how you angle them. He explains, 'I try to keep all the cameras as low to the ground as possible, because as soon as you go up in the air you make all the jumps look so much smaller. Whenever people actually walk around the course and see the fences for the first time, they all react the same way and say "Gosh – isn't it enormous!", so it's important for us not to diminish the size and impact of the fences.'

The week before the event the BBC moves in, starting to build the camera platforms, as each camera has to work off a perfectly flat surface to produce good quality pictures. Then they start laying the cables, thousands of feet of wiring that will carry sound and pictures from each location back to one of two mobile control rooms. In some places they go underground through specially laid ducts, in others they're hoisted overhead on scaffolding bridges, and in one or two cases the lines are threaded through the jumps themselves. By midweek the huge, distinctive green outside broadcast vans have rolled into place, bringing the thousands of pounds' worth of recording and transmission equipment needed for the Saturday and Sunday transmissions. Any material to show the atmosphere and preparation for the competition before Saturday is shot by a small mobile crew of just a cameraman and sound recordist, and is certainly the least complicated ingredient in the whole process.

On Friday night there is a final check to ensure that everything is in place and working. Johnny Wotherstone sits in the hot seat in the main control vehicle checking that each camera is sending pictures and sound, that everyone can hear his directions, and those of his assistant producer in the second control van in the Vicarage fields. They work methodically through the checklist of recording and transmitting equipment; the computer that holds all the information on the riders and will provide relevant captions throughout the two days; the timing equipment provided by Seiko to give vital information on speed during the cross-country phase. They check that the dozens of television sets provided by Radio Rentals and placed around the course for the public, in the competitors' tent and in Frank Weldon's office, are all receiving pictures from the control room on a closed circuit link. Throughout Saturday these televisions will carry the continuous output from the thirteen cameras so that no matter where you are as a spectator you can get the broad overview of what is happening on the whole course. On Saturday morning the entire checking process is repeated once the crowds start arriving, to make sure that thousands of pairs of feet have not disturbed the cables or equipment. The commentators are installed with microphones and monitors to keep them abreast of events and by noon the whole machine is ready to swing into action the moment the first rider comes to the end of the final phase of roads and tracks ready to set off over Frank Weldon's impressive thirty-two fence course.

The commentary team is now a trio of Hugh Thomas and Mike Tucker, two riders who have brought their skill in and knowledge of the sport to the microphone, and Raymond Brookes-Ward, who progressed from being the lad in 1972 to work alongside the late Dorian Williams. Raymond makes no claims to

Above: Captain Mark Phillips clear through the Coffin on Columbus, 1979.
Right: The Queen congratulating Princess Anne on winning the Armada dish in 1980.

being an expert on eventing. Instead he says that his role is definitely that of the journalist. 'I reckon my big job at Badminton is trying to signpost the interesting stories so that when we join Grandstand the viewers know what's been happening while they've been away watching football, golf or whatever.' He walks the cross-country course three times before the Saturday, 'because you have to identify the fences and their location immediately', and he prepares for the competition all year round by picking up information about various riders and horses and entering it in a small notebook. It is something he started doing when he first went to Badminton in the 1950s, for as he says, 'There wasn't a lot of information around at the time. We didn't have a press officer for Badminton like we do now in Jim Gillmore.' Information alone, though, does not make a good commentator. It is knowing when to talk and when to shut up, being able to stay calm in a crisis – and in live television, the crises are the trickiest part of the job. Raymond remembers one year standing in the competitors' starting box, having just done an interview with one of the riders, when the producer, who was then Fred Viner, suddenly said through his earpiece, 'We're coming to you live for commentary on Virginia Holgate's ride'. 'I was nowhere near a television set and didn't have a clue what was happening, but we were on the air so I started to mumble something about "She's going well" when Viner said to me, "Can't you come up with something a bit more interesting than that?" when he must suddenly have realized that I couldn't see a thing. So he gave me a running commentary over my earpiece, and I just kept talking while I gently made my way across the starting box until I could see a television. It was nerve-racking, but I don't suppose the public ever realized what was happening.'

Years before, Dorian Williams had demonstrated his unflappability when someone opened the door of the commentary booth as he was in the middle of a live transmission. He had been leaning against the door, and so fell out of the booth onto the grass. But he just kept on talking, and all the engineers noticed was a slight hiccup in his voice as he hit the ground. In telling the story himself, Dorian added a postscript. Apparently, that evening he was called to Badminton House to be confronted by the Duke and the Royal party. Princess Margaret had heard the commentary, and suspected that Dorian had tripped or fallen over in some way and wanted the truth 'straight from the horse's mouth'!

Each of the three commentators currently employed has a clearly defined role. Hugh Thomas works mostly from the starting box with the roving camera, where he can interview riders and eventing personalities at key moments. Raymond is installed in the official commentary box in the corner of the show jumping ring, where he works directly off the pictures on the television screen – and never sees a rider actually jumping a fence. During the afternoon he is joined by Mike Tucker, who is usually competing at Badminton as well as commentating. That makes it a hectic day for him, but it brings an invaluable extra dimension to the commentary as he can describe what is happening based on his own experience.

The avid viewer at home can see coverage during Saturday's Grandstand plus an hour of live action and recorded highlights on BBC 2 at about 4.30 p.m. There is another hour on Sunday afternoon of highlights from the previous day, and then the closing stages of the show jumping, when the winner finally emerges – about two and a half hours in all. To achieve that coverage, everything that moves on the cross-country course is recorded, from the first competitor plunging out of the starting box to the last horse home and dry. Some things are recorded twice – taking a section in slow motion, for instance. And while the main action is being recorded on a master tape, the video editors are constantly updating an edited version of highlights. It is all a case of the hand on the video machine being swifter than the eye. For when the Grandstand presenter says, 'Let's go to Badminton live', what you actually see is a combination of live coverage of whichever horse is on the course at that moment, plus recorded highlights of those competitors who have ridden earlier, so viewers miss none of the day's most exciting action.

It means that by the end of Saturday the producer can have up to eight hours of competition on tape, more than enough to prepare the recorded package for the following day's programme. Overnight five cameras are moved into the main arena to cover the show jumping, while the rest of the equipment is packed away and returned to London, Glasgow or wherever. The whole operation is scaled down on Sunday to cover the closing stages of the event. It becomes a fairly straightforward operation of recording the show jumping, editing, and being ready to put the programme out, live from the showground, at about 4.30 p.m. From then on most of the crew can relax, as the drama is over. But in 1976 that was the very moment when the greatest drama of all was about to begin. A jubilant Lucinda Prior-Palmer had won the event for the second time. She was riding Wide Awake and was waiting to begin her lap of honour after the presentation. Most of the cameras were switched off, and Raymond Brookes-Ward was just thirty minutes away from introducing the programme, live on air. Suddenly Wide Awake plunged forward, reared, and within seconds dropped dead. Says Raymond, 'That was the worst moment of my life. It was shattering. No one felt like being happy or gay, but we had to go ahead with the programme. There was no way that we could open our transmission by saying that the winning horse was dead. So I went on air having to do all the bright, happy, chatty links saying what a marvellous Badminton it had been, in a few moments we shall start the show jumping, but before that let's look back at the dressage ... have a look at the cross-country ... the show jumping commentary was already recorded, and then they came back to me in vision for a complete change of style to say, "I'm terribly sorry to have to tell you that a few moments ago Wide Awake collapsed and died." I never want to have to go through that again.' It was a unique, one hopes never to be repeated situation. But Johnny Wotherstone admits that as with all 'live' events he has to be prepared for the tragedies as well as the triumphs, and his attitude is uncompromising. 'We never show a horse in distress. If it happens, cut the shot, go to another camera, it doesn't matter what, anything, but get away from it. Then if the horse is all right, you can come back and show that it's OK, if not, then you update the situation verbally ... but no, you never, never show it.' Happily, the situation is a rarity, and most people have only the warmest of memories at Badminton.

For Raymond Brookes-Ward it was seeing the sheer pleasure on the Queen's face when her horse Columbus won in 1974, ridden by Mark Phillips. For Johnny Wotherstone it is simply being there. 'It is,' he says, 'a lovely thing to do. It's what it stands for, the history of the thing, and the prestige. It's also a very picturesque thing to cover and a lovely place to work.' For others it is perhaps the memory of spectacular falls, or fluid, faultless performances from horses and riders. They are all moments that have been captured on the small screen, bringing the pleasure and unique spirit of this competition to millions.

Top: Jane Gundry, Badminton Horse Trials Secretary.
Centre: The Duke of Beaufort with competitors in the 1986 championship at the Badminton stables.
Bottom: Sweeping up the gravel before the first vet's inspection.

7

BEHIND THE SCENES

Ask any of the thousands of spectators who go to Badminton each year to sum up what the competition is all about, and most would say 'horses'. But in the single-storey building in the centre of the village identified by the weatherbeaten sign as the Badminton Horse Trials Office, they will tell you that for 95 per cent of the year what Badminton is really about is people, and paper. Hundreds of the former, mountains of the latter, and not a horse in sight.

A sporting event the size of the Whitbread Championships is not put together in a few weeks, or even months. It is a year-long process that has been honed into a slick, effective operation over more than twenty years of quasi-military rule. With so many former majors, colonels and assorted ex-Army personnel associated with the event, it is not really surprising to find that the whole thing is run with the precision of a huge military exercise. The bulk of the year's administrative work falls on four sets of broad shoulders. Those of Colonel Weldon himself, of course, his assistant director and treasurer, Major Derek Dyson, Jane Brookes in the box office, and the event secretary, Jane Gundry. Between them they maintain, steer, drive, and successfully deliver the leviathan that is the Badminton three-day event. The 'operations manual' (and no event of this size could operate without one) is affectionately known within the office as the 'Bible'. No one can remember when it was begun, but the consensus is that the whole organization would be lost without it.

Jane Gundry is the keeper of the 'Bible', a large blue exercise book containing the name of every person to be contacted, every job to be done, and meticulously lined into a giant graph to plot the progress of work throughout the year. August is a fallow time in the office, when most people take their holidays after settling the accounts, writing all the thank you letters, and generally mopping up after the event in April. It is in September that the whole machine is taken out and oiled in readiness for the nine-month drive to the next championships. Out in Badminton

Park, Frank Weldon and his fence builders are preparing the ground and cutting the timber for the new course, while in the office Jane begins the mundane but essential job of ordering the mountains of paper that will be needed for printing and duplicating every kind of letter, information sheet and application form. The first of those letters start going out – to the contractors who supply the catering and public address system, the acres of tentage, the staff for the car parks, the electricity and the temporary roads.

Every year letters are sent inviting tenders from the same people. As Jane explains, 'We don't like changing our suppliers once they've got to know our system; that way the whole thing runs relatively smoothly'.

Anyone who has ever tried to book into hotels or guest houses in the vicinity will know that everything within a twenty-mile radius of Badminton village is booked solidly for the week of the competition months in advance, so one of the first jobs for the office is to arrange the accommodation for the three judges who are both the ground jury and the dressage panel, and without whom the competition simply would not be official. It is also a time for deciding whether any increases are to be made in the price of tickets and trade stand accommodation. The income from the trade stands produces a major chunk of the Badminton profits, and Derek Dyson has seen a steady increase in demand for space, regardless of mounting annual costs, while Jane Brookes, and her mother Joan Petre, who ran the box office for twenty years, both maintain that 'no matter how expensive you made the seats in the grandstand around the royal box, you'd still be sold out within a week'.

Nevertheless, there is no point in raising the fees to ridiculous levels, so new charges are set after numerous consultations between the various departments and careful calculations that compare cost to profit ratios. That is when Weldon prepares for his one and only committee meeting. His feelings about committees in general are uncompromising, and well known within the Badminton organization. 'The ideal committee,' he states, 'consists of just three people, one of whom is away ill and a second who can't make the meeting, leaving just the old fool [pointing to himself] to make all the decisions.' The Badminton committee is listed in the front of the official programme. In fact there are nine names, not three, including the Duke of Beaufort, Major Ronnie Dallas, who has responsibility for the stabling, Major Laurence Rook, who takes charge of the dressage arena, and Richard Wood representing the accountants, as well as the regular Badminton office staff. Yes – they do all attend an official committee meeting, during the first week in October, and yes – there is an official agenda. But as Ronnie Dallas says, 'Frank tells us what he's decided and what he's going to do. We all agree, and then let him get on with it. The whole thing never takes more than three-quarters of an hour, and it works perfectly.' This is a tribute not just to Weldon's organizing ability but also to what Laurence Rook describes as his 'sheer genius for finding the right person to do the job, and then being able to walk away from it and let them get on with it.' To a large extent this is true, but it does not take long for a casual observer, like myself, to notice that no matter how efficient any individual might be at his or her allotted task, the rider is always added to their decisions and actions that what they've done is final 'provided that Colonel Frank agrees'! And once he has agreed, the Badminton bandwagon begins to gather momentum.

It is in October that the weekly magazine *Horse and Hound* carries the first advertisement for the competition, announcing the dates and ticket charges and

Huntsman Brian Gupwell with the Duke of Beaufort's hounds in front of Badminton House.

informing would-be spectators that the box office will be open for business in January. The printers begin work on application forms and tickets, and with Jane go through the annual ritual of choosing a colour for all the official badges. It is changed every year so that people cannot claim privileges to which they are not entitled, and as there are only a limited number of colours available, it is not as straightforward as it sounds. Jane calls it her 'multicoloured jigsaw puzzle'.

As the weeks progress and the trees in the park change from late summer green to a riot of autumnal shades, the Badminton village Post Office deals with an increasing flow of mail to and from the event office. Advertising space in the official programme is sold, and trade stand applications despatched and returned. Every letter and answer is carefully logged in its appropriate column in the 'Bible'. The format is always the same. Anyone who took advertising or trade space the previous year is invited to do so again. If they decline, then the invitation goes out to whoever is next on the waiting list. A few people do drop out for various reasons; only on very rare occasions are individuals 'struck off'. 'It certainly happened once,' recalls Derek Dyson, 'when one of the exhibitors had a blazing row with the director and told him to "★+#! off".' I guess he didn't realize who he was talking to, but he was never invited back.' Certainly those incidents are the exception rather than the rule, and as most trade exhibitors are anxious to maintain their presence at Badminton, by November Dyson is able to start compiling the master plan for the shopping area.

On his office wall he keeps a scale plan of the commercial area and has a stock of small markers representing 10 ft, 20 ft, 30 ft and 40 ft shop fronts. As the applications start arriving he places the relevant shop onto the map. Most stands like to have the same spot each year so that regular customers know where to find them – unless, that is, they are in the Park Piece away from the main stream of commercial activity, in which case they jump at the chance of being resited in 'Bond Street' should the opportunity arise. Each stand is colour coded depending on what it has to sell; saddlers, for instance, would be blue, clothes shops red, charities yellow, food stalls green, and so on. It means that Dyson can see at a glance if there is a heavy concentration of one type of shop in any given area, and re-adjust the plan accordingly.

By this stage the office is filled with the clatter of typewriter and duplicating machine, and the telephone constantly ringing. Another, rather incongruous sound, is added to the daily clatter – a sewing machine. Jane admits ruefully, 'I should never have let on that I knew how to sew'. But she did, and now every September finds herself making a selection of flags in red, white and blue. They're the warning flags issued to every fence steward on cross-country day. In an emergency they wave the appropriate flag to call for a doctor (red), the vet (blue) or the fence repair team (white). Their use is backed up by a highly efficient radio and telephone network, but the flags give immediate visual location above the heads of the crowd to whichever of the three services is required. During the rest of the year the flags are often lent out to other events, along with the stewards' whistles, so in September they are recalled, and if necessary repaired or renewed.

Throughout the winter months the empty pages of the 'Bible' are gradually filled with the notes and cross-references that record the steady progress towards championships week in April. Rosettes and plaques are ordered – getting the number right is always a gamble, because apart from the main winners, everyone who completes the course receives a special white rosette and a shield bearing the name of the competition and the date, and even though previous years give some idea of the percentage of riders likely to finish, the decision is still largely guesswork.

There is no such gamble involved with Armada dishes – the small, highly prized silver mementoes presented to every rider who has completed five Badminton competitions. The recipients are worked out from the records collated at the end of each event; the dishes, engraved with their names, are ordered in November, ready to present the following year.

The paperwork goes relentlessly on. Frank Weldon finalizes the schedule and entry forms for competitors, and sends preliminary invitations via the British Equestrian Federation to the various overseas federations who might like to send competitors, and accommodation is tentatively booked for the two dozen or so foreign riders who will certainly accept the invitation.

At one time all overseas visitors were installed in the sanatorium of the nearby girls' school at Westonbirt as the event coincided with their spring holidays, but now Jane has to rely on a few local hotels and the growing number of bed and

Above: The Quarry, 1985.
Left: Team work constructing the Bullfinch.

breakfast establishments. At least one useful by-product of the change is that the office now has a substantial list of local accommodation, which is sent out with tickets to help those spectators who want to stay in the area for the whole three or four days.

Details are finalized for supplying prizes from the Worshipful Company of Saddlers and the National Light Horse Improvement Society, and for building the temporary pedestrian bridge that links the coach park and steeplechase course with the main competition area.

Just before Christmas details of special coach and party rates are sent off to the BHS headquarters at Stoneleigh so that they can be included in the various spring newsletters for Pony Club and riding club members. Badminton's press officer, Jim Gillmore, sends off the second, and largest of the advertisements to *Horse and Hound*, and in the office all the typewriters and duplicating machinery are serviced so that everything is raring to go after the holiday.

On 2 January the Badminton bandwagon moves up a gear, and begins a gentle but perceptible acceleration towards April. Sue Ingal joins the permanent office staff, and begins by sending out publicity material to over three hundred tourist and information centres in Britain, while several miles north of Badminton, just outside Cheltenham, the box office opens and establishes its first contact with the general public.

The vast majority of spectators still just turn up on the day and pay their car park fee at the gate. But anyone wanting to guarantee a seat in the 6000-seater stand, to watch either dressage on Thursday and Friday or the show jumping on Sunday, has to book in advance. For twenty years, from 1965, Joan Petre ran the office from the spare bedroom of her home. In 1985 she handed over to her daughter, Jane Brookes, who also works from home, and between them mother and daughter have perfected a system that makes the box office run as smoothly and efficiently as possible.

Each year everyone who writes to the office to book a ticket in advance is recorded in a master file, and given a reference number. The following year they are automatically sent application forms in the first post of the new year – some 4000 letters. On 15 January the box office opens for business, and begins processing the 200 or so letters a day that start arriving in response to the *Horse and Hound* advertisement, as well as the mailed application forms. After the initial rush, the post trails off to a steady fifty of sixty letters a day but it all adds up to more than 3500 advance bookings, each one demanding a different combination of options, from a full season ticket, including car pass and grandstand tickets for dressage and show jumping and a caravan park site, to individual tickets for specific days.

They come not just from Britain, but from all over Europe, Australia, New Zealand and America. Mrs Petre recalls taking barely £300 in ticket money for the whole competition in her first year. Now it runs into six figures, with the pattern of sales giving a clear indication of the way in which interest in the sport has developed. 'There was a colossal surge in applications the first year Princess Anne competed,' she says, 'and more recently we've noticed more people taking an interest in dressage.' But according to both mother and daughter one thing will never change, and that is the number of people wanting to book seats next to the royal box in the grandstand for the final day. 'We could sell those seats a hundred times over,' they say, and apparently get letters from people actually asking that their seats should be 'as close to the royal box as possible so that I can get a good view of the Queen'.

While the flow of mail continues out of the box office in Cheltenham, back in the main office in Badminton village they are on a carefully calculated fifteen-week countdown to the championships.

The Avon and Bristol Federation of Boys Clubs is approached to provide an arena party to build the show jumps on the final day, and a florist is engaged to provide flowers for the directors' tent and the royal box. The highly complex electrical timing equipment is ordered to provide accurate and immediate results from the timed sections of the speed and endurance day and the show jumping phase, while final orders go off to the printers for cocktail party invitations and for meal ticket vouchers for the grooms, who will be provided with free meals in the cavernous kitchens at the rear of Badminton House. The grooms are also given free accommodation, either above the huge permanent stable blocks or in caravans that are requisitioned in January and parked in a field behind the main office the week before the competition starts.

Top: The farrier, Bernie Tidmarsh at Badminton 1986.
Below: Rodney Powell with horses, grooms and
equipment before setting out for Badminton in 1986.

Above: Diana Clapham and Jet Set, 1984.
Left: Strong muscles are requisite for grooms!

Anyone who has ever driven to Badminton, especially on cross-country day, will not have to be told that getting a car in or out of the site takes a combination of planning and patience. Over 20,000 vehicles pour off the motorways and main roads to squeeze themselves into the tiny Gloucestershire lanes on that day, and keeping them moving is a major undertaking shared equally between the police, the AA and National Car Parks. In January the Traffic Committee meets in the village hall to discuss tactics. For the police it is a combined operation, shared by the Avon and Somerset and the Wiltshire constabularies, who have seen a pattern emerge over the years that gives them a clear picture of what direction the traffic is coming from, and the peak hours when most people are trying to get in or out of the showground. To keep a steady flow they have identified eight major routes, which are signposted by the AA a week before the event, each one leading to a specific car park where the attendants are briefed to keep the traffic flowing. The simple equation is that the faster you can park the cars, the less time they will spend backing up along the lanes, and the less chance there is of a monumental holdup.

Out on the course the fences are still taking shape, but by now Frank Weldon knows exactly where each obstacle will be, so he is able to draw up the official map giving the location and number of each fence and the rider's route around the course, the steeplechase phase and the roads and tracks. He also writes to the many volunteers who will head the various sections such as medical, veterinary, timekeepers and communications, asking if they are once again prepared to give assistance, and organizes the voluntary staff to help them. Meanwhile two of his 'lieutenants', Major Geoffrey Bowden and Major Laurence Rook, begin organizing the many judges and stewards who will be needed during the four days.

The dressage arena is Laurence Rook's responsibility, and it takes only a handful of stewards to ensure that the event runs smoothly and to time. Geoffrey Bowden, on the other hand, is responsible for over a hundred and twenty judges, assistant judges, stewards and 'command post' personnel to man the steeplechase and cross-country fences. Most are recruited from the famous 'Blue Book', the membership list of the Beaufort Hunt. It can be a thankless task sitting out in the middle of a field, more often than not getting frozen to the marrow by the wind and rain, just watching a procession of more than seventy horses jumping over the same obstacle. But the judge and his stewards are a vital part of the cross-country machinery. It is their judgement that decides whether or not a rider has had a refusal or a fall, has collected any penalties, has ridden the correct side of a marker flag, should or should not be eliminated for an infringement. The stewards, assisted by the mounted stewards who are also from the Hunt, have to keep the course free of pedestrians to give the riders a clear run at each fence, telephone the score through to the main control room and keep a clear head to summon the right sort of assistance in an emergency. Many of the volunteers have been regulars at the competition for years. But as some retire new recruits are brought in, and these have to begin by serving an apprenticeship on the steeplechase course, where the fences are relatively straightforward. Once they have proved their ability on that section, they are 'promoted' to the more complex demands of the cross-country course, first as a steward and then an assistant, and finally, as vacancies arise, as a judge. It may all sound a rather officious way of treating people who are after all 'volunteers', but the judge's decision at each fence is final, and is therefore crucial to the result of the competition. There is a complaints procedure but it is rarely called into action, so the judges have an enormous responsibility to make accurate decisions and it is Geoffrey Bowden's first responsibility to ensure that his staff are up to the job.

The timekeepers also have to bring a totally professional attitude to their work, and the group of volunteers who fulfil that role are the only ones who are not taken from the Beaufort 'Blue Book' or the immediate neighbourhood. They are drawn from the ranks of official timekeepers used by the Amateur Athletics Association and various amateur cycling clubs . . . which is how they have been given the affectionate name of 'trick cyclists' by Weldon. They are approached in January to give the organizers time to fit Badminton in with the various marathons, track events and cycle races that they will also be asked to supervise during the season. They use the very latest electronic timing equipment and mini computers, backed up by the old fashioned mechanical stopwatch. Perhaps because Weldon himself was once almost certainly robbed of a title through inaccurate timekeeping, the director ensures that this aspect of the competition is handled by experts, with nothing left to chance.

With still the best part of two months to go, Jane Gundry and the printers establish the layout for the official programme. The centre portion is always the same, containing the map, the drawings of the fences and the buff-coloured pages that carry the score sheets and index of entries. As none of that can be finalized until all the entries have been processed, that section is left until barely three weeks before the event. But the rest of the seventy or so pages can be assembled, with photographs, information relating to the event and the advertisements, for a print run of 40,000 copies.

In 1978 a new feature was included – the first of Frank Weldon's now regular, highly informative articles headed 'The psychology behind this year's cross-country course'. In these five pages he describes in detail many of the fences,' the alternative jumping options, the problems that he is setting the competitors, and the degree of horsemanship he is looking for to negotiate the course successfully. Weldon claims it was only put there in the first place to give him five extra pages on which to sell advertising space. There is certainly a degree of truth in that, as the programme is designed to have an advertisement on the left hand page faced by some form of editorial on the right; clearly that commercial necessity has produced what for many spectators is one of the most valuable sections of the programme. In between juggling with the contents so that she's not left with an empty page, and proof-reading every word, which she does quietly at home away from the mounting bustle in the office, Jane Gundry still has to work through the list of mundane but essential jobs contained within the master timetable of the 'Bible' – like applying to Avon County Council for permission to build the temporary pedestrian bridge over one of their roads and to change the flow of traffic through the village, as well as ordering the various dope-testing kits required by the vets. Even equine athletes don't escape the stringent international laws on taking 'illegal substances'!

During February there is a constant two-way flow of communication between the office and potential competitors. It starts as just a trickle in January, but then sets into full swing as riders apply for entry forms and then return them with their £45 entry fee and proof that their horse has achieved the necessary qualifications to enter the competition. At this stage, for the very first time, the horses begin to feature in the process.

With the cross-country course virtually finished, the BBC makes its first appearance, in the guise of the senior outside broadcast producer and engineer, who are given a guided tour by Weldon to discuss camera positions and technical requirements for what will be a massive media event. At about the same time Caroline Bromley-Gardner, the artist responsible for the line drawings of the fences, gets her first view of the course. Her drawings give the only complete view of the course for many of the spectators who never have the opportunity of walking the whole string of thirty-two fences. As a rider herself, she draws each fence from the rider's viewpoint, and explains, 'It means that the spectator can see the fence as the riders will on their approach'. Occasionally she takes a slight bird's eye view, as the more complicated fences can look like no more than a jumble of rails from the ground and give no idea of the shape and design of the obstacle at all, and occasionally fences are drawn from the side to give the full impact of a drop or a ditch, which you certainly would not see from the front at the Normandy Bank or the Coffin, for instance. As with so many things at Badminton, the drawings are such an obvious visual aid to spectators it is hard to believe that they were not always there. In fact they did not appear until 1968. The previous year both Caroline and Weldon had seen a similar idea used in the programme for the 1967 world championships at Punchestown in Ireland. As her father, Lt.-Col. R. Bromley-Gardner, was Badminton's assistant director at that time, it did not take long to turn what was clearly a good idea into a regular feature of the Badminton programme. An initial pencil sketch made on site is turned into a detailed and accurate pen and ink drawing, complete with marker flags showing the left- and right-hand side of each element – a vital indicator for riders and spectators alike in the more complicated combination fences. Caroline has to work quickly, getting her drawings to the printer by the end of March, and as the course changes direction each year and always includes new and modified fences, there is little opportunity for reusing previous sketches.

Frank Weldon admits that he avoids office work as much as possible, preferring to delegate to other capable hands. But as the event draws closer his role as administrator becomes more and more demanding. There are fairly straight-forward things to do, like conferring with the Duke on who should be invited to the cocktail party, and dictating letters to the people who will receive complimentary passes for the event – people like the wives of former directors, officials from other horse trials and major equestrian bodies, and those who have given exceptional service to Badminton over the years. Once the competitors' list closes he compiles the short biographies that accompany the name of every horse and rider in the programme, and makes the draw to establish the running order for the first two phases of the competition. In theory this is done by picking the entrants' names out of a hat. In practice, Weldon takes the list home one evening and returns the following morning with the completed draw. 'There's no secret about it,' he says. 'All it takes is a couple of whiskies and a fairly concentrated couple of hours work.' While pulling names out of a hat might seem to be the fairest way of conducting the process, it simply would not work in practical terms. Any rider entering two horses has to be given a substantial break between the two rides, so their positions have to be carefully plotted. It is also important to have a few good riders going early to prove to the rest that the course really is jumpable, and likewise to have top-class names at the end of the draw to ensure that the championships maintain a level of interest and genuine competition right to the last moment. Once those criteria have been met, the rest can indeed come out of the hat.

Organizing publicity for the event is the responsibility of newspaperman Jim Gillmore. During the championships he will be shepherding and acting as central information point to over 300 reporters and photographers from all over the world. Not just the equestrian press come to report the event, but representatives of the national and international populars, who descend *en masse* as Royal-watchers and have probably never even see a horse, let alone photographed one. In the weeks and months leading up to the competition he organizes the official advertisements and supplies regular press stories involving key figures and developments relevant to the championships. With near-capacity crowds rolling up on each day once the event is in progress, it might seem unnecessary to promote it even further. But hundreds of thousands of people with an interest in the sport never get a chance to visit it in person, and like to be kept informed about its progress and outcome. It is a constant source of disappointment and wonder to Gillmore that in spite of Britain's phenomenal success in the sport internationally, and the level of public interest it attracts, so few of the popular press bother to feature eventing in general, and Badminton in particular, on their sports pages. He says ruefully, 'A fourth division football match gets more coverage than an international three-day event championship'. His is a constant battle to achieve a higher press profile. Frank Weldon, as a journalist himself (a former equestrian correspondent for the *Guardian* and the *Daily Telegraph*) knows the value of publicity, and is a willing interviewee whenever Badminton is likely to benefit. In March he and the Duke host a press day when reporters and photographers are invited to come and look at the course, talk about it, and photograph the Duke and Weldon at any of the more interesting fences. It alerts the public to the sort of competition to expect, and might even persuade some of the more reluctant sports editors that this really is an event worthy of greater national press coverage.

At about the same time Major Ronnie Dallas, secretary of the Beaufort Hunt, and Brian Hingham, the Duke's stud groom, begin to organize the stable routine. The magnificent stableyard behind Badminton House will take eighty horses in the style and comfort associated with an age of class and privilege, when the stables were as much a showpiece as the house itself. In addition at least another dozen stables are prepared in buildings surrounding the main square to provide total accommodation for up to ninety competitive horses. For most of the year the Duke's own mounts and those of the Beaufort Hunt are stabled in the square. Before the event horses arrive the regular inmates have to be found alternative stabling or grazing, and their stalls are scrubbed down to prevent any risk of infection. Bedding – a choice of straw, shavings, or peat – and forage are ordered, and are all supplied free to competitors, a unique facility of the championships. It is confirmed that the farriers will be available from Wednesday until Sunday, and also volunteers who will man the competitors' lorry park and the stable office to deal with the enquiries and needs of individual riders.

For eleven months of the year the Badminton estate is a working farm, providing grazing for sheep, cattle and horses, as well as a permanent herd of deer. In recent years the deer have been kept within an enclosure, well protected from the effects of a quarter of a million members of the general public. But several weeks before

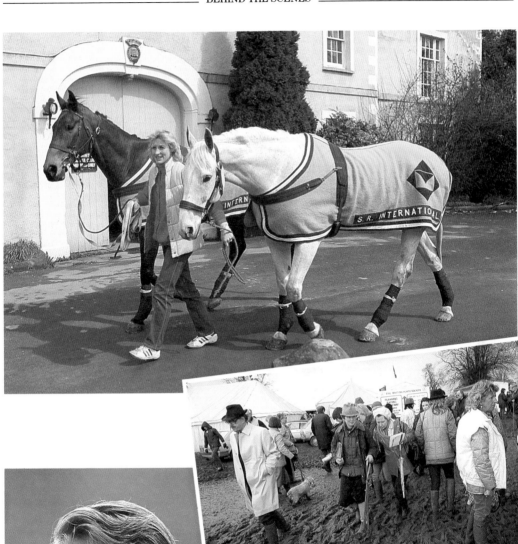

Top: Lucinda Green arriving at Badminton 1986, with
Shannagh and Count de Bolebec.
Centre: The hazard of mud in 1986.
Bottom: The Duke of Beaufort.

Top: Inside the magnificent stables at Badminton.
Left: Strike-a-Light (USA) takes a rest, 1986.

the event the rest of the stock is moved well away from the main centre of activity, while most of the estate workers and tenant farmers begin cleaning the waggons and trailers that will be pulled into place around the Lake, the Quarry and other fences, to provide grandstand views for thousands of spectators.

Considering the size and international importance of this event, it is amazing just how many of the facilities are provided through goodwill. Apart from the trailers, at least thirty local farmers offer their Land Rovers, usually with themselves as drivers to take the press and officials around the course on cross-country day, or to be positioned at various points around the course as emergency vehicles to carry doctors, vets, or fence repair teams. Like the rest of the formidable army of volunteers, the only thing any of them gets out of it is a free pass to the event and an invitation to the Duke's cocktail party.

As March draws to a close Badminton Park begins its transformation from elegant parkland to a commercial showground. Contractors begin to erect tents to house the shops along 'Bond Street', following the detailed instructions taken from Major Dyson's master plan. The huge framework of the grandstand begins to take shape, and over a matter of days the grass disappears under the temporary metal roads, the mobile display units and caravans, the temporary toilets and catering centres and the tracery of cables carrying electricity, telephone links, the public address system, and the BBC's miles of camera cables. The competition affects, and involves, just about everyone in Badminton village. The vicar lends the field behind the vicarage as an extra lorry park, ladies from the village supervise the toilets and sell programmes, tractor drivers stand by to pull cars, lorries and caravans out of the mud when it rains, and the small village shop stocks up with a lorryload of extra supplies to feed the influx of people who more then double the village population for four days. Michael and Janet Luter took over the small village store in 1966, and say that their first Badminton was a novelty, but by the second year the novelty had worn off; and now they can face the week as something to enjoy. Two weeks before the extra customers descend on them they buy huge stocks of cigarettes, wine and beer, and the sort of staple foods that are easy to cook on small caravan stoves, such as pies, sausages, chops and steak. From Thursday to Sunday the shop is full from 6.30 a.m. until 10 o'clock at night, for although many of the meals are provided free, competitors often prefer to eat in their own caravans, and the spectators who fill the public caravan park look for a daily supply of milk and groceries that are piled into the Luters' family van and taken around the site as a mobile shop.

One commodity they keep in bulk, and supply free of charge, is ice. After the cross-country run some horses may need a cold compress or icepack to help ease a swelling or bruise, and the Luters are always happy to provide bags of ice to wrap around the horses' legs. This small but significant contribution yet again highlights the way in which this Gloucestershire community make it their event.

In the main office across the road from the shop, Jane Gundry and Sue Ingle are working flat out to send off some 500 car passes and official badges to every one of the volunteers, and to the trade stand exhibitors and hospitality marquees, who automatically receive a quota of free passes depending on the size of their stand.

With a full ten days to go before the start of the championships every one of the jobs detailed in the 'Bible' should have been completed – every letter written, every job apportioned and every detail of administration and organization attended to. It leaves a breathing space to answer queries, solve any problems that crop up and prepare the administration needed actually to run the event from day to day.

As Jane Gundry says, "This operation is a bit like a snowball. It goes on getting bigger and bigger until you think the whole thing will just burst. Then in the last few weeks, with luck the worst of it is behind you, and you know the headache is nearly over. That's when we can start loooking forward to the thing we've all worked so hard for – and really enjoy the competition.'

The shopkeepers Michael and Janet Luter at the Badminton village stores.

8

THE EVENT

To call Badminton a three-day event is not only something of a misnomer, it also completely underestimates the true scale of the operation for both the organizers and the competitors.

To the public the timetable is clearly defined. Dressage on Thursday and Friday, speed and endurance on Saturday, with show jumping and result on Sunday. A nice, tidy, four-day package containing all the sporting elements of expectation, challenge and triumph.

But in 1986, when I spent months observing the work of the Badminton administration and talking with riders, it became obvious that it is difficult to define a single day on which preparation ends, and the event as such actually begins, even though officially the competitive element of the Championships ran from 17 to 20 April. Riders were arriving two, even three days before the first day of dressage, while the director and his full-time staff rarely paused for breath.

To observe and absorb the unique spirit of this annual event, I joined the Badminton team on Sunday 13 April for the beginning of a week that was to be filled with drama and tragedy, soaring hopes and jubilation and the downright spiteful behaviour of the English weather. Sunday was not an arbitrary choice. It is on that day that the Park is opened to the public, who can walk and inspect the fences of the championship course, and when the bulk of the huge army of volunteer officials are given their instructions.

By 10 a.m. the village hall was filled with the green Barbours and assorted tweed jackets and caps of more than a hundred cross-country judges and stewards. Each of them clutched an envelope containing a car park pass, a map of the course, and an invitation to the cocktail party. In addition, the judges were given their 'kit' of whistles and emergency flags, a stopwatch, and a specimen scoring book, which explains exactly how to mark each rider at individual fences. Once Geoffrey Bowden, who is in charge of stewards, had done the roll call to make sure that none of his troops were missing, Frank Weldon ran quickly through the rules and

Previous page: Rachel Bayliss on Mystic Minstrel at Horsen's Bridge, 1982.
Top: Three of Badminton's best-known faces – Major Laurence Rook, Colonel Frank Weldon and Major Derek Dyson.
Left: The Director, the Duke and the ground jury at the competitor's briefing in Badminton village hall, 1986.

scoring procedure, delivered a few brusque words about the proper use of the telephone when giving scores or calling for assistance in an emergency, and then sent them off to familiarize themselves with their allotted fences.

At the more complicated, combination fences Weldon gives each judge an individual briefing. He points out the area of the penalty zone, which is clearly marked by a row of pegs. Once the riders enter that zone, if they fall, stop or have a refusal they incur a set of penalty points, and they may not 'cross their tracks' inside the zone when making an approach to any element. The judges are shown where they can park their Land Rovers and position themselves to get a clear view of the fence in order to make accurate judgements. At fences where the riders have a choice of routes the judges have an extra responsibility, to time each competitor through the fence and to indicate the route they took. Several weeks after the competition Frank Weldon will scrutinize these calculations to make sure that riders taking the bold, fast route through the most difficult part of the fence really are rewarded with a time advantage over those who choose the slower, easier routes. If the judges' calculations show that in fact some of the easier routes are just as fast, then Weldon looks for ways of ensuring that they really will be much more time-consuming the following year. That is why, a few years ago, he introduced the rather complicated series of rails alongside fences like the Lake, the Stockholm and the Coffin, so those taking the easier option do add several vital seconds to their overall time as they thread their way through the barriers.

At each fence Weldon carefully explains the demands of that particular obstacle, and patiently answers any queries or anxieties. The cross-country scores are the most decisive of the competition, so it is vital that the judges feel confident and absolutely certain of their responsibilities.

On the steeplechase course the fences, and therefore the instructions, are much more straightforward. The stewards are reminded to check the fences carefully for damage after each circuit. One year a pole was dislodged, and was left sticking out like a lance towards the chest of the following rider, who spotted it only just in time. It is an unhappy reflection on society, rather than the event itself, that at the morning briefing a detective sergeant spends a few moments talking to the meeting about security precautions, a message brought home on the steeplechase course, where the stewards are advised to keep an eye on the central command point – the bus that houses officials and time keepers – and the public toilets, just in case there are any suspicious packages left lying around.

Throughout the morning of the briefing it rained steadily, and at lunchtime there was much discussion about the long-range weather forecast for the week. The optimists maintained that it was bound to get better. But those who had tuned into the farming forecast shook their heads and prepared for the worst.

After lunch Major Ian Castle met his staff of a dozen timekeeprs and stopping stewards to talk through their responsibilities on cross-country day. While the 'trick cyclists' and their highly sophisticated timing equipment will record the actual time taken to ride the steeplechase course and the cross-country fences on Phase D, every one of the four phases of the speed and endurance runs to a meticulous timetable. Every rider knows exactly at what time he or she must start each one of the four phases that make up the speed and endurance test on Saturday. They also know that arriving late at any of the checkpoints, and taking longer than the allotted time for any phase, will incur time penalty points. So at the start of each section a timekeeper and official starter carefully send each rider off at precisely his or her alloted time, while other officials log the time at which the four finishing lines are crossed. In addition, there are two stopping stewards, positioned one third and two thirds of the way round the cross-country course. If there is an accident or some emergency that means a rider has to be stopped on the course, one of these stewards will stand in the middle of the approach to their nearest fence, and prevent the next rider from continuing. He makes a careful note of the length of time that rider is held up so it can be deducted from that

competitor's overall score at the end of the day. Riders must obey their signal to stop; if they do not do so they are eliminated – a rule that was brought in after one well-known lady rider totally ignored a stopping steward as she approached the Half Moon fence in 1985. As that was one of her 'bogey' fences, she did not want to hang around getting even more anxious about it before being allowed to jump so she just sailed on, and pulled up before the Lake, a fence she found less terrifying!

By late Sunday afternoon it had stopped raining. A few hundred locals were walking their dogs and their children around the course, taking advantage of 'fence Sunday', while many of the volunteers were catching up with friends they had not seen since last year's Badminton and reminiscing about previous competitions. There were hair-raising stories about riders almost, and occasionally actually, colliding with spectators in the days before the route of the course was roped off and strictly 'policed' by stewards, and I had an admission from one of the timekeepers that one year in the early 1960s the master clock on the cross-country course got fractionally slower and slower as the day progressed. When the timekeepers realized what was happening, they made slight adjustments to all the times based on calculations from a set of reliable stopwatches though it was almost twenty years before they had the courage to admit to Frank Weldon what had happened!

On Monday morning Jane Brookes and her mother Joan Petre moved the box office, lock, stock and barrel, from Jane's house near Cheltenham into the main Badminton office. Two weeks before the 1986 competition every grandstand seat for Sunday's show jumping was sold, but the box office is always open throughout the competition to sell any remaining seats and to deal with the hundreds of enquiries that crop up over the four days.

The stableyard behind Badminton House was practically deserted. Most of the

Left: Diana Clapham and Jet Set at the Arrowhead, 1984.
Above: The President, ridden by Lucy Bywater, 1984.

regular hunt horses had been moved out to make way for the competitors. Only a dozen or so were left, rugged up and munching in their stalls, to provide mounts for the Duke and his house guests during the week. The remaining eighty or so boxes stood empty and waiting, smelling of freshly laid shavings and straw, the brass hooks and bolts shining in the welcome morning sunshine and the sounds of Radio One echoing through the vacant buildings, while the grooms busied themselves with the daily routine of stable chores.

In contrast, the trade area was alive with activity, and the air filled with the staccato rhythm of hammer on wood as floorboards and exhibition stands were persuaded into place. There were delivery lorries and workmen everywhere. Within hours ground that had been merely soggy for weeks was relentlessly churned by lorry and tractor wheels into ruts, then a morass, and finally isolated paddy fields. Most of the tented shops were empty, but a number of large mobile display units, especially those belonging to saddlers, had already arrived, ploughed their way into position, and had staff laying out their goods. The ground was so wet it was impossible to walk anywhere without Wellingtons, and tractors were already heaving caravans and cars and a large BBC van through the glutinous mud in what was clearly an unwelcome portent of things to come.

Later that evening, standing in front of the house and looking out on the deserted park and the tented village there was a surreal feeling about the scene, because the crowds were missing. Everything else was there – the shops and the fences, the

flags, the potted flowers. An event waiting to happen – a bit like Harrods must be just before the main doors are opened on the first morning of the sale.

There was time to draw breath and enjoy the quiet of the moment before the tidal wave of humanity rolled in and brought the scene to life.

In the stableyard a clatter of hooves heralded the first arrivals. The Dutch rider Eddie Stibbe was anxious to give his horse Autumn Venture a chance to stretch his legs after the ferry journey across the Channel and long drive from the coast. Just behind him, Susan Ritchie with her mount Winter Sun drove into the yard after a seven-hour drive from Cleveland. It was her first Badminton, and she wanted to give her horse plenty of time to recover from the journey and get used to the new surroundings. 'We don't expect to win,' she told me 'but we qualified, so we're here, and that in itself is an achievement. Every fence we get over will be a bonus.' A sentiment that would be shared by many of the riders following her into the yard over the next twenty-four hours.

Because the two horses had arrived so early none of the official vets was there to check them over, so they were put into temporary 'quarantine' stalls for the night, and looked at first thing on Tuesday morning before being officially housed. Every horse arriving at Badminton has to be checked by the vet before going into the main yard. Their passports are scrutinized to ensure that they are fully vaccinated and that the horse registered on the documents really is the one in the lorry. Once they have been passed and identified they can be bedded down in their appropriate stall.

From early Tuesday morning there was a constant flow of horseboxes, lorries and trailers through the main street to the village hall and the vets' inspection, then back through the cottages, past the hunt kennels and into the unloading area in front of the stable courtyard. In the stable manager's office – a small wooden hut in the corner of the yard – stud groom Brian Higham supervised the stabling of the horses and handed over the good luck telegrams and cards that had already arrived. Out in the competitors' lorry park Dick James was treating the vehicles like Lego blocks, packing them in tight formation and achieving a minor miracle in parking – especially now that a number of sponsored riders turn up in huge liveried waggons that not only carry the horses but also include comfortable living accommodation. While the grooms unload all the equipment that they will need to see them through the next six days, and stack it in neat piles outside the appropriate stall, the riders saddle up and take their horses on a quiet stroll around the Park. It gives the horses a chance to stretch their legs after what may well have been a long road journey, and the riders get a long-distance view of some of the course. Officially they are not allowed near the fences until after their official briefing on Wednesday morning, but they cannot ride through the Park in blinkers so the occasional outline of rails on the skyline gives a tantalizing hint of what is to come.

As if to complete the scene of stately home with horses on the lawn, just after lunch kennel huntsman Brian Gupwell appeared, walking thirty couple of Beaufort Hunt hounds across the park to the lake. The hounds had been hunting until the previous Wednesday, and Brian was keen to keep them exercised. It would be impossible on Friday and Saturday, so he was making the most of a fairly quiet day in the Park. Down by the lake the estate workers were pulling two farm trailers into position to provide extra seating for the thousands who would position themselves at that fence all day on Saturday, and were deciding who would be able to supply tractors to pull cars out of the mud. It had rained solidly all night, and the showers during the day had been intermittent but vicious. The trade stand area was already a quagmire, even before several thousand pairs of spectators' feet had got to work on it, so all the signs were that this was going to be one of the wettest, muddiest Badmintons for years and the 'troops' were laying down contingency plans, preparing for the worst.

Back in the stableyard the rhythmic metallic clang of hammer on anvil was coming from the farrier's shop in the far corner of the courtyard. Inside, farrier Bernie Tidmarsh was working on his first customers, Michaelmas Day and Any Chance, the mounts of Olympic gold medallist Mark Todd. As Bernie explains,

Left: The well-travelled lorry of Dutch rider Eddie Stibbe.
Right: The Duke of Beaufort's hounds.

'When the riders are fully stretched travelling around the competition circuit, they don't always have time to get their horses shod for Badminton, especially by someone they trust. And that's what I'm here for.' He's been 'here' at Badminton for seven years, taking care of the hunt horses throughout the season and working with most of the well-known event riders based in Gloucestershire. For the championships he is on call every day to deal with what he calls the 'daily maintenance' as well as emergencies.

By 6.30 that evening the rain clouds had disappeared, and the mellow Cotswold stone of Badminton House and its stables was bathed in the soft light of unexpected evening sunshine. All but four of the competition horses had checked in and were snugly bandaged and rugged, the rows of grey,.chestnut and bay heads either tucking into haynets or dozing quietly while their human attendants sorted out their own accommodation in the grooms' quarters and caravans, the lorries and local hotels. Meanwhile, the three members of the ground jury were giving their verdict on Frank Weldon's cross-country fences. Vicomte Jurien de la Gravière from France, Mr Anton Buhler from Switzerland and Dr B. Springorum from Germany had arrived at Heathrow airport earlier that day. These three men not only judge the dressage phase but are also the official body responsible for overseeing the entire competition. Once they arrive, responsibility for the competitive element of the championships passes out of Frank Weldon's hands and into theirs. Their inspection of the course not only ensures that none of the fences go beyond the dimensions of maximum height and spread allowed, but also that in design and layout the obstacles present a fair test worthy of international status. Their reaction, as it always has been, was both positive and complimentary, so Weldon attended Wednesday morning's competitors' briefing confident in the knowledge that there were no last-minute adjustments or alterations needed to his carefully designed course.

The riders' briefing at 10 a.m. in the village hall is an obligatory meeting, even for those who have been to Badminton before. It is an opportunity for the Duke to welcome his 'guests'; for the riders to identify the ground jury; and for Weldon to remind competitors of the rules of the competition and to add his regular lesson on good manners. It is the same message every year. 'Remember that you're guests in the Duke's stables. Respect his hospitality and don't let your horses wander where they shouldn't, especially through the daffodils in the front drive.'

With the homily delivered the meeting is over, and the riders make a dash for the door, collecting their copy of the programme and a map of the course, on their way to the lines of waiting Land Rovers and assorted four-wheel-drive vehicles. With Weldon in the lead the convoy moves off to drive round the first three phases of the speed and endurance test so that everyone can become familiar with the route they will have to take through the woods and plantations for the roads and tracks, and round the nine fences on the figure-of-eight steeplechase course. There is always a certain amount of jostling among the riders to be in the first vehicle behind Weldon's familiar old Land Rover, and on the more open sections of the route many display a dash and nerve behind the wheel that reflects their boldness in the saddle as they jockey for position, bumper to bumper. At the end of Phase A – the first part of the roads and tracks – the riders pile out of their vehicles for a quick briefing before being sent off to walk the steeplechase course, with a gruff instruction from Weldon to 'get a wiggle on' as he is anxious to finish the tour

Virginia Leng (née Holgate) on Night Cap II, 1985.

before lunch. Just before setting off on Phase C, the second part of the roads and tracks, Weldon indicates across the Badminton airstrip, which runs parallel to the steeplechase course, and points out the section of Phase C that crosses some of the Duke's fields. 'In theory you can ride right across those fields,' he says, 'but in practice I suggest you stick to the edges. If you don't you'll never ride at Badminton again.' The warning is given with a grin, but no one doubts Weldon's word for a minute.

I had hitched a ride in the Land Rover with American rider Torrance Watkins Fleischmann, and her countrywoman journalist Kitty Wieschkoff. This would be Torrance's second ride at Badminton. The first was, she admitted, the 'biggest course I've ever ridden over in my life', and she was full of praise for Weldon's fences. 'It's no good going round a course thinking to yourself "What on earth has this course builder tried to do – break my neck?" That affects your confidence, and the horse's. This course is bound to be big, but I have great respect for Weldon's judgement.' Kitty believes that 'Weldon builds this course to test the best of the British'; and considering the few overseas riders who have won here, she could be right.

Our driver was John Woolridge, who with his wife Lesley looks after the public caravan park. His family used to live in the house that is now the Petty France hotel on the main road at Dunkirk. In the 1950s the roads and tracks used to cross the main road near their home, and while Torrance was anticipating that this would be the loneliest part of her day, with an hour or more of hacking through the muddy

Ricenda Lord weighing up the Huntsman's Hangover fence, 1986.

tracks and byways, John recalled that at least one of the early riders used to arrange a little stop off at their house half way round the course for a tot of warming whisky – confirming just how much more relaxed the atmosphere was in those early days.

At the end of the route the convoy made its way back into the main area of parkland, behind the grandstand, to the starting box for Phase D. At that point most of the seasoned riders went off to exercise their horses or to begin walking the cross-country course. For the newcomers there were more instructions from Weldon, explaining the procedure in the box during the compulsory ten-minute halt before riding the final phase, and a warning that the whole area would look quite different on Saturday, with many of the landmarks that were obvious in the deserted Park being obliterated by the thousands of spectators. 'And I promise you,' he added, 'that the great British public might want to watch you risking your neck over the fences, but they won't always get out of your way when you're making your way through the crowds to the box. Many of them will be so busy drinking beer and eating their sandwiches that the last thing they'll expect to see is a horse.' This might sound a rather ungenerous statement coming from a man who does, after all depend on the support of that 'great British public' to make the competition a success – but believe me, he's absolutely right.

As the riders drifted off in twos and threes to walk the course, six grooms from the hunt stables were busy with brooms and buckets, sweeping the gravel off a long strip of concrete in front of Badminton House. Later that afternoon every one of the competition horses would have to be presented to the ground jury and the senior vet to ensure that they were fit and sound to enter the championships. At one time this inspection was done in the stableyard, but the crowds of spectators have grown so much over the past few years that in 1981 the location was moved to the front of the house. A permanent concrete strip was laid to give a smooth, flat surface on which to run the horses, and for most of the year it is covered by the gravel drive. Under Brian Higham's eagle eye every chip of gravel and drop of surface water was cleared so that no horse could be wrong footed on the all important 'trot up'. As the riders arrived back in the stable from their initial view of the course, the general reaction was unanimous. 'It's big and demanding, and likely to be made more so if the ground gets any wetter.' There were anxious exchanges about how to approach some of the fences, with the Ski Jump getting particular attention. Most riders will walk the course at least three, if not four times before they ride it, to plan their approach and route through the obstacles, with a few alternatives up their sleeves should the conditions, or previous riders' problems, or even their own anxieties about their horse, call for a sudden change of plan on the day.

Before they even get close to jumping the fences, however, the horses have to be passed by the veterinary inspection panel, which was in position and ready to receive the first horse by 5 o'clock. They presented in numerical order, each horse plaited and groomed to shining perfection, with owners and grooms fussing over them to the very last moment. When their number is called, the rider presents his or her horse to the panel, standing calmly while four sets of eyes expertly scan these equine athletes. On a signal the horse is walked away from the group to the end of the concrete run, and then trotted back. If all is clear there is a nod from the senior vet, Frank Mahon, a nod from the Vicomte as president of the jury, and a discreet thumbs up from Laurence Rook to Ronnie Dallas, who announces over the public address system, 'Horse number one . . . passed'. The relief from the attendant humans is tangible, as is the anxiety of the waiting riders. Those four little words can make or break ambitions even before the competition begins, so no matter how confident they may be of their horse's fitness there is always a degree of tension. And sadly, not everyone gets the 'thumbs up'. Number 43, the grey gelding Nifikim, was never brought out of his stable, having pulled a muscle that afternoon, while American rider Bruce Davidson had an agonizing few minutes as the panel asked him to trot J. J. Babu no less than three times before finally giving him the all clear. Jane Holderness-Roddam was less fortunate; the second of her two rides, Ebony Green, was 'spun' when deemed lame by the panel, as was Claughton, who had made the trip from Humberside with Nick Harland. As the crowds dispersed and the successful riders focused their minds on their dressage tests, Claughton and Ebony Green were taken to veterinary consultant Bill Walter, who was on duty in the stableyard. He confirmed that Ebony Green had a tender shoulder – a mystery to Jane, who knew he had been sound throughout the day – while Claughton seemed to be sore in the foot. In the smithy Bernie removed the horse's shoe and the vet confirmed the early warning signs of an infection. In spite of their size, horses are notoriously delicate creatures, and there must be an element of Murphy's Law that guarantees they will go lame the very minute you are convinced they're fighting fit and raring to go. Whatever the crazy logic of the situation, by 6.45 p.m. the competition was already over for three horses, and even knowing that there will be other years is poor consolation for their riders and owners.

As the sun was setting and the shadows lengthening in the Park, there were typewriters clattering busily in the secretary's tent. On Wednesday morning, immediately after the riders' briefing, Jane Gundry and her staff moved their operation out of the village and into their temporary tented office close to the main scoreboard, giving them a central position from which to control operations. As soon as the vet's inspection was over, secretary Sue Ingal began typing out the lists which gave the riders their dressage starting time, beginning at 9 a.m. and continuing throughout the two days at ten-minute intervals until 4.20 p.m., with timed breaks for coffee, lunch and tea.

As the sheets were being delivered to the competitors and the press tent, the last of the trade exhibitors were stocking up their stalls, and looking anxiously at the ground outside. What should have been an avenue of cropped green grass was a sticky mess of brown mud. Stories were circulating about the mayhem in the caravan park, where three tractors had been working flat out since 1.30 p.m. towing cars and caravans into position through mud that was axle deep. The vicar was having hysterics at the sight of his one and only paddock being ploughed into furrows by lorries that slewed and skidded their way over boggy turf. And as the evening news forecast even more rain to come, the first of the rumours and anxious questions began . . . would Weldon cancel? Out came all the old apocryphal stories of how the last time Cambridge won the boat race coincided with the last time the event was cancelled . . . and of course Cambridge won in 1986! Uncertainty and doubt rumbled steadily through the night. The only person apparently totally untroubled by any of the speculation was Weldon himself. With his trilby hat pulled firmly over his eyes, and his face set in a sardonic grin, for him it was business as usual, and to hell with the rain.

The first rider into the dressage arena at 9 a.m. on Thursday morning was Katie Parker, not a competitor but the 'guinea pig' rider, who gave the three judges in their individual boxes an opportunity to mark each movement in the test and see if all three were working to the same standard, not producing a huge disparity between the scores. After a brief consultation, the three men returned, each to his own wooden hut, and the first rider of the competition, Lucinda Green on Count de Bolebec, was waved into the arena by a bowler-hatted steward at precisely twenty past nine. The competition was at last under way, and right on cue the rain began a steady, relentless downpour. The day before, Lawrence Rook and his gardener had managed to mow the 60 by 20 metres arena to give a good surface for the test, and several years ago the whole area was underpinned with skelpings to improve the drainage. Britain's spring was proving a severe test of the ground, but while the collecting ring degenerated into a morass, the dressage arena stayed relatively dry. The ground began to cut up as each competitor trod the same ground in the ritual of loops and straight lines, but at least the horses were not moving hock deep in gluey mud, and the judges marks were soon reflecting the excellent standard of horsemanship being displayed on this first day.

There are twenty movements in the championship dressage test, each one marked out of ten points; an extra four categories for the general impression of both horse and rider gives a possible maximum of 240 points from each judge. The final mark is reached after a complex process of addition, subtraction and multiplication. As each rider completes the test the score sheets are collected from the individual judges. The three sets of 'good' marks are totalled and divided by three to give an average. This average mark is deducted from the possible total of 240, and the resulting figure has a factor of 0.6 added. This new total is then

The magnificent backdrop of Badminton House.

subjected to the 'multiplying factor' which can range from 1.5 to 0.5, depending on the severity of the cross-country course. At Badminton in 1986 it was set at 1.0. When the ground jury inspected the cross-country course on the Tuesday afternoon they assessed the degree of difficulty presented by the obstacles. A really severe course would have the higher figure applied to it so that the dressage marks would reflect quite a difference between the best and the worst of the riders. This multiplying factor also ensures that the dressage marks do not have too great an influence on the overall result, keeping the ratio between the three elements of the competition to 3:12:1, that is, dressage influencing three parts of the total, speed and endurance 12 parts and show jumping one.

Getting these scores right needs a cool, analytical mind – in other words, a computer. But true to the traditional atmosphere of the sport, the computer was not introduced into Badminton until 1985, and even then it was carefully watched over by its human counterpart, senior scorer Janet Hill. For years she has done the whole process 'manually' – a *tour de force* of mental arithmetic, helped by a series of tables that add the coefficient and multiplying factor to every conceivable average score. The computer now does all the complicated mathematics and automatically prints out the scores in order of merit, but even so Janet still does the whole process herself as a double check before entering the scores for each section of the competition on a series of colour-coded charts – giving an instant card index on the performance of each competitor. Frankly, championships of this standard are too important to leave to the tender mercies of a machine, especially as in its first year of use the BBC accidentally disconnected their mains cable and wiped out the entire computer memory half way through the competition!

As the riders presented themselves to the judges in a procession of top hats and tail coats, with horses bursting out of their skins with energy in anticipation of the major cross-country test and yet demonstrating just how balanced, supple and obedient they can be, the scores were processed, and passed on to the press tent, the secretary's office, the BBC, and the giant master scoreboard in the centre of the main trade avenue, where George Bishop carefully painted in each total in the appropriate box next to the name of each horse and rider. Several riders, like Polly Schwerdt and Robert Lemieux, were taking valuable time out with their trainers to polish up a few movements before going into the competition arena, while at least one rider, Ginny Strawson, was reluctantly packing up to go home. Her horse, Sparrow Hawk II, had gone lame, and there was no point in carrying on.

At a press conference that afternoon Frank Weldon welcomed everyone to 'this little gymkhana in the Duke of Beaufort's front garden', and confirmed that Whitbread would remain as sponsors until 1988. When one of the pressmen dared to ask, 'As this is your twenty-first year, how much longer do you intend to carry on?' Weldon's face reflected the noncommital tone of his answer, 'Maybe next year . . . maybe not. Who knows?' and that was an end to the discussion. Queries about the effect of the rain on the course were dismissed with equal alacrity, with Weldon reminding his questioners about the careful preparation of the ground on both the takeoff and landing side of each jump. 'The course is fine,' was his verdict, but you could understand the concern by just looking at what was happening to the Duke's 'front garden'.

Early that morning, while the first riders were performing their dressage tests to a virtually empty grandstand, the commercial avenues were already thick with people. The steady action of thousands of green wellies was puddling the mud into a runny mess that got deeper and stickier as the day progressed. Incredibly, few of the spectators realized how destructive their feet were being out on the course as they walked from fence to fence, meticulously following the exact route of the horses down the middle of the roped route, creating a muddy track as clear to follow as any yellow brick road. At least it had not rained all day, and a late afternoon breeze was beginning to dry the surface. As people prepared for the evening cocktail party, rumours about cancellation receded. And then the heavens opened. Not just a shower, but a rainstorm of monsoon proportions. Inside the panelled reception rooms of Badminton House the champagne and compliments flowed as positions at the end of the first day of dressage were confirmed. Virginia Leng and Night Cap II were in the lead with 42.20 points; a crop of familiar names filled the top ten placings, with young Claire Mason, riding in her first Badminton on The Artful Dodger, neatly placed in third position.

Twenty-four hours later, when the rest of the riders had completed the dressage phase, there was a new leader, American Bruce Davidson scored an unbeatable 40.60, Ian Stark and Sir Wattie had moved into third place, and Lucinda Green had ridden one of her best tests ever on the grey Shannagh to give them fourth place

Right above: Duncan Douglas and A Touch of Class at the Elephant Trap, 1983.
Right below: Former world champion Bruce Davidson (USA) on JJ Babou, 1982.

*Opposite page top left: David Green on
Super Salesman at the Zig Zag, 1984.
Top right: Mark Todd on Charisma at the
Catherine Wheel, 1984.
Bottom: Chris Bealby on Jack-be-Nimble,
1978.
This page top: Chris Collins and Gamble,
1980.
Right: Virginia Leng on Night Cap at the
steeplechase, 1986.*

overall. In fact, the top twenty placings included, as you would expect, some of the outstanding names from the sport, and encouragingly a number of young riders clearly marking their cards as future contenders. In spite of Bruce Davidson's pole position, the atmosphere in the American stable block where the three USA competitors were housed, was tinged with gloom. Torrance Watkins Fleischmann's grey gelding Tanzer had pulled a muscle in the sticky, deep mud in the collecting ring just minutes before she was due to ride her dressage test, and she had had to withdraw. Badminton was to have been her last ride, a 'warm up' before flying to Australia to represent her country in the world three-day event championships, but this represented more than just a competitive setback. Tanzer was, in her opinion, 'the biggest, bravest horse I've ever ridden', but he did not belong to her. Badminton would have been their last ride together, as in May the horse was being returned to its owners in Maryland. It was a tragic way to end their partnership.

Mud had claimed its first victim, and there were those who felt that it might eventually claim the entire event. Anxious stallholders just wanted to know one thing: 'Is it on, or is it off? Why doesn't someone make a decision and tell us?' Throughout Friday the public had continued to pour in, creating a two-mile traffic jam on the main approach roads, and turning the car parks and trade areas into a commercial version of the Somme. Paradoxically, it is Badminton's enormous popularity that threatens it when the weather is bad. Weldon knew that, barring a flood, the course would be fit to ride, so there was no question of cancelling from the competitors' point of view. But a quarter of a million spectators on the Saturday, and the cars they arrive in, can cause havoc with the parkland when the going turns to mud. In previous years Master had been adamant that the Park should not be destroyed, which is why the championships were cancelled in similar circumstances in 1975 when the ground became a mud bath by Friday evening. The new Duke is more phlegmatic in his attitude, knowing that modern farm machinery and techniques can heal the ground far more quickly than was possible a decade ago. So extra tractors were put on standby, and after consultation with the ground jury Weldon reaffirmed what to him had been obvious all along: 'We go ahead ... no question of stopping now.' I recalled the message he had drummed home to his stewards at the Sunday morning briefing when running through the procedure for stopping the cross-country phase in an emergency. 'Don't hang about,' he said, 'keep the machine running' – he was obviously the first to follow his own advice.

Despite Weldon's confidence in his course, many competitors were less certain. All day long they were walking and rewalking sections of the course, knowing that what was fine to jump in dry conditions posed quite a problem in the wet. The two youngest horses in the competition were withdrawn, the eight-year-old Glenburnie, Ian Stark's second ride, and Newfield, Karen Straker's second horse. In both cases it was felt that it would be unfair to put the young horses over the big course in what were far from ideal conditions. A fright now could ruin them for life. So although both were well placed after the dressage (Glenburnie was tenth, Newfield twenty-third) they would have to wait another year to face the fences.

Several of the riders were not all that happy about conditions for their more experienced horses. What dismayed many was the way in which literally thousands of people were churning up the ground on the takeoffs and landings as they examined every detail, every nail and inch of bark on the obstacles. Frank

Lucinda Green wades through mud before the dressage.

Weldon's 'skelpings' may well have created perfect drainage on each side of the fences, but the constant erosion caused by the Wellington-booted curious had stripped the ground of every blade of grass, leaving sticky, muddy patches at the very point where the horses would need all the stability they could get. At the Ski Jump, a pretty formidable fence to begin with, the great British public had surpassed themselves. Apart from stripping the approach slope bare, some children were tobogganing down the steep slope towards the bottom rail as if it really was a ski slope. Eventually the course builders fenced off the approach with a set of chestnut palings, but the intrepid still managed to get on to the slope and wear the turf bare. Aware of the anxieties, the ground jury had reinspected the course at 5 o'clock after completing the second day's dressage. They were satisfied with the state of the ground, and gave Weldon his go-ahead.

That evening the sky was dark apricot, streaked with orange and purple, perhaps not quite the right colour to invoke the old saying 'red sky at night, shepherd's delight' but it was near enough the right shade, and it *was* at least dry!

The Saturday morning of the Whitbread Championships has all the tension and electric atmosphere that accompanies any gladiatorial event. In the stables the order of the day is quiet routine. Horses are fed, mucked out, groomed, and the early runners tacked up in preparation for their ride. Willing helpers pack together the equipment and spares that will be needed out on the course during the day, while trainers and family talk through the fences with their riders, keeping them calm, giving them encouragement. The whole object of the exercise is not to make the riders any more nervous than they already are. But horses have never learned about the stiff upper lip. While their riders try to ignore the churning in their stomachs and the mounting apprehension, the horses know no such inhibitions. They pick at their feed, stamp and move around their stalls impatiently, or stand shaking with anticipation. Every fibre in their being proclaims loudly what their riders' stoic faces try to conceal – that this is the big one, and the next few hours could be among the most important of their lives.

Beyond the stables Badminton Park has been a hive of activity since before 7 a.m. The police and car park attendants were ready for the onslaught, and by 8 a.m. the first intrepid spectators were examining the fences, and a few had even settled themselves in the prime position on the grandstand by the edge of the lake.

In the few hours until 11 o'clock, when the first horse was due to begin the first phase of the speed and endurance, each of the dozens of individual components were preparing themselves so that once started, the 'machine' could run continuously and smoothly.

BBC technician and production staff began their final checks to see them through what would be a five-hour recording session, punctuated by live transmission into BBC 1 and BBC 2 sports programmes. The young nannies from the Norland Nursery Training College were laying out the toys and equipment needed to look after the babies and small children left in their safe hands during the competition. By 10.30 all 180 members of the Red Cross were mustered outside their hospital tent close to the main control box. The Red Cross provide doctors and nursing staff throughout the four days of the championships, but on cross-country day, as with so many other voluntary helpers involved in the organization, they know that extra facilities and personnel are required. For organizational purposes the cross-country course is divided into five sectors, plus the steeplechase course. Each sector has a central control point in radio contact with Frank Weldon's headquarters and is assigned a doctor, vet, fence repair party, communications personnel (from the Royal Wessex Yeomanry) and a full complement of Red Cross attendants for each fence, backed up by Red Cross Land Rovers and a team of paramedics. Inside the central Red Cross tent, where they have all the facilities of a small field hospital, a staff of doctors, nurses and Red Cross members are ready to cope with any medical emergency affecting competitors or members of the public. In the past they have had everything from heat stroke to broken bones, premature childbirth and heart attacks. At least one ambulance is kept on standby to rush serious cases to nearby Frenchay Hospital in Bristol. The year prior to the Los Angeles Olympics the medical officer for the Games came to Badminton to see how the Red Cross organized its coverage on cross-country day. He left in awe of the voluntary enthusiasm and boggled by the scale of the operation, convinced he would never be able to match their efficiency and effectiveness.

In addition to the human ambulances, there are also the horse ambulances – long trailers hitched to Land Rovers – the vehicles no one wants to see used. For it is absolutely true that although no one ever wants to see any of the competitors injured at Badminton, somehow spectators can come to terms with human casualties while an injured horse is anathema. Between 10 and 10.30 a.m. the steeplechase and cross-country judges and stewards are in position next to their appropriate fences, complete with telephone links to HQ, whistles, flags, score sheets, and axe or billhook to slash through the ropes supporting the poles should a horse get caught up in the fence. Only the Stockholm fence judge does not need an axe. He has a JCB standing by, as the log over the ditch could never be moved without one!

While the fence judges test and establish their telephone links with the central scoring office, over which they will give verbal confirmation of success or failure as each rider goes through to back up their written score sheets, the men of the Royal Wessex Yeomanry check through the radio links for their involvement in the operation – codenamed Exercise Rideaway. They are connected to the HQ communications centre, where the commentators and Frank Weldon will watch the careful progress of each competitor round the course. They do this via a simple though ingenious contraption, known as the Trotter board because it was devised by a former Yeomanry officer, Colonel W. Trotter. The board is a section of timber, marked off rather like a ruler with each stage of the speed and endurance test. The first section is marked roads and tracks, then there is a line for each of the nine fences on the steeplechase course, a further section for Phase C (the second part of the roads and tracks), one for the ten-minute halt in the box, and then marks for every one of the thirty-two cross-country fences, each one numbered and named. The officers who operate the board have a series of cards giving the name of each

Sue Benson on Bally Valley, 1983.

The Red Cross team ready for action in the hospital tent.

rider and horse and their competition number. As the riders set out at the start of Phase A, the card is slotted into a small brick a little like a children's playbrick, which is put on to the top of the Trotter board, ready to be moved along as the appropriate messages come in from the outlying radio controllers, who are based at the start and finish of each section of roads and tracks: on the steeplechase course, where one man can see the whole course from a central position, and from vantage points all round the cross-country course.

Their remarks are short and concise, to prevent congestion on the airwaves. The simple statement 'fence five, horse ten, clear' is enough to send the wooden block on down the board to the next fence. If a rider falls, or collects penalty points, that information is added to the block. In the control room it is a silent operation as the competitors have their ride plotted down the board. The only remarks come from the commentators, who can see at a glance exactly how many horses are involved in each stage of the test and the state of their progress round the course. If there is an accident or emergency, it gives Weldon the only complete picture of the course on which to plan his strategy.

Under the huge chestnut tree on the edge of the 'box' close to the start of Phase D, Lady McMeekin is giving last-minute instructions to the members of the Duke of Beaufort's Hunt branch of the Pony Club – the young riders who will scamper through the crowds carrying the written score sheets from fence judges back to central control throughout the afternoon. At each of the start and finish points the timekeepers are carefully checking their watches and electronic timing equipment.

While the public pour into the park in their thousands from the M4 and via Stroud and Malmesbury, filling the shops or securing vantage points on the course, Weldon's 'machine' is meshing together, cog by cog, ready to burst into life when the first competitor rides out of the starting gate. For Weldon himself there is little to do by mid morning but watch and wait. At 9.30 a.m. he had given final instructions to the fence repair teams before setting off on his rounds to check each sector and ensure that everyone had arrived and was in position. For the rest of the day he would be in the control box. Like any good general watching his troops perform, he would intervene only in an emergency.

Overnight the first two horses on the starting list had been withdrawn, Lucinda Green's Count de Bolebec and Madeleine Gurdon's Midnight Monarch II. So the first horse on the course was to be Night Cap II, ridden by Virginia Leng, winner in 1985 on Priceless (who later in 1986 became world champion). A huge crowd had collected around the starting box for Phase A just in front of Badminton House, in good time to watch one of Britain's most popular lady riders set out on the course. While Night Cap was quietly walked around the base of the magnificent chestnut tree in the centre of the starting box, bandaged and rugged to keep his muscles warm, Ginny checked her stopwatch and carefully taped the paper giving start and finish times for each section to her wrist. In the weighing-in tent she stood on the scales with her saddle. All riders have to carry a minimum weight of 11 stone 11 lb – not difficult for most of the men to achieve, but something of a problem for many of the lady riders, who usually have to carry extra lead weights in their saddle cloths. A large kitchen clock tied to the wooden post at the starting line showed the time approaching the first 'off' as knots of friends and helpers, grooms and trainers all fussed over horses and riders.

At precisely 11.08 a.m., with rider, trainer and official timekeeper all synchronizing their watches, Ginny and Night Cap calmly trotted over the starting line on the first phase of the speed and endurance test. There was nothing dramatic about the start; the dash and power would come later, in Phases B and D. All that is required to begin with is a steady hack to cover just over two and a half miles in twenty minutes. Even before Ginny had left the crowds by the Lodge to enjoy the temporary peace and quiet of the tracks through the woodland, the second rider, Petrina Philpot, was already circling on Mr Panache. And so it would continue throughout the day, with riders setting off at four-minute intervals right up until 2.56 p.m., when Ian Stark and Sir Wattie would be the last combination to start.

Night Cap completed Phase A with several minutes to spare before jumping the steeplechase circuit. The support teams were already in position ready to meet the first riders and check over the horses. Crowds stood four deep on the rails around

Janet Hill, the chief scorer, confirming results with the Badminton computer.

the circuit. Many had poured straight out of the hundreds of coaches parked below the airfield, and were getting their first sight of the competitors. Watching with equal interest from the starting box were a number of riders, including Bruce Davidson and David Green. They were both due to ride much later in the day, and wanted to see how the overnight rain had affected the going on the course. Mike Tucker had time to watch only one rider around the course before dashing back to the BBC outside broadcast unit to prepare a recorded package for later in the day, then ride the course himself at 2 o'clock and round off the day with live commentary for BBC 2's transmission at the end of the afternoon. Anyone who questions the lunacy of that timetable gets one of Tucker's lopsided grins and the characteristically flip answer, 'Well, it keeps my mind off the competition.'

In the old double-decker bus at the rear of the starting box the two sets of official timekeepers were ready for the first competitor. At 8 o'clock that morning they had dug a discreet trench across the course to lay the cables for the electronic beams that would trigger the start and finish of each ride. Cliff Franks and his team would be supervising the electronic equipment, while Frank Harrington and an assistant would provide a backup system with mechanical stopwatches. The following day Cliff would be one of the official timekeepers for the London Marathon, while Frank has been timing athletics events for thirty years, and was one of the officials to clock Roger Bannister's first four-minute mile. Clearly their credentials are impeccable, which is why these days Badminton is one of the few international events that rarely, if ever, faces controversy over official timings.

Ginny and Night Cap flew around the steeplechase course at a cracking pace, and as she landed over the last fence and broke through the electronic beam, the small computerized clock chattered out the official time onto a paper roll and showed what the mechanical stopwatches confirmed, that she had completed the course in just under the optimum time of four and a half minutes. So no time penalties to add, as she brought Night Cap back to a walk and eased him into Phase C – the second stage of roads and tracks. The second horse was already on the course, well clear of the second fence, with the third rider just arriving in the box. And so it would go on, for almost four hours, now that the conveyor belt was in full swing.

It takes forty-five minutes to complete Phase C, a six and a quarter mile stretch that runs parallel with the A46 and A433 before turning right at Worcester Lodge and onto the avenue that, in more elegant times, was the main carriage drive into the house. During that time the riders have to keep checking their watches, making sure that they maintain a steady 220 metres per minute. If they go too fast, they will take too much out of the horse before the final, most strenuous phase, but they cannot hang around either, and risk picking up penalty points if they go over the optimum time. While the riders are clockwatching, the support teams are racing back from the steeplechase course to the Phase D starting box to be ready to spring into action during what is always referred to as the 'ten-minute halt', but at Badminton is in fact an eleven-minute halt.

During the break the horse will have its girth loosened and be checked over by a vet to make sure that it is not unfit or unsound in any way. Once it has been passed, the 'team' will begin greasing the horse's legs with Vaseline or lard to give further protection and lubrication should the legs come into contact with the solid timber poles. While one half of the team administer to the horse, the other half are busy

Susan Blane on Kalambu at the Normandy Bank, 1982.

giving moral support and encouragement to the rider. Once a few competitors have gone around the cross-country section, trainers and helpers can give the riders valuable information during the halt about how particular fences have ridden and where unforeseen problems may have cropped up. A rider may even have a chance to nip into the competitors' tent in the middle of the 'box' and watch a few fences being ridden on the closed circuit television feed from the BBC. When you are the first rider out, you are very much the pathfinder, having to rely totally on your own judgement and reading of the course, knowing that the rest of the field will reap the benefit of your mistakes and triumphs.

Out on the course, the gathering crowds count the minutes down to 12.28, when the first rider would begin the cross-country. Although before even reaching this section the riders will already have been competing for an hour and twenty minutes, it is the twelve minutes and twelve seconds it takes to jump those thirty-two formidable obstacles that is the real focus of attention. All the drama and real heart-stopping excitement of the afternoon will take place in that arena. That there is an element of risk and danger involved adds spice for the spectators but inflicts agonizing attacks of nerves and sick apprehension on even the most seasoned competitors. Once it is all over there will be exhilaration and relief, but during that compulsory halt there are monumental exercises in self-control

going on, and the atmosphere is tense and electric.

With three minutes to go the riders are usually in the saddle, girths tightened and checked, anxious to get on with it. The official starter counts down the time to the 'off'. Two minutes, one minute, then it's just seconds. 'Ten, nine, eight ... three, two, one, Go!' And without exception the horses plunge in an explosion of power and energy out of the starting box and across the line on their way, slightly down hill, to the first fence.

While the riders and their mounts get on with the job of negotiating each obstacle, their supporters make a dash for the competitors' tent, squeezing in among the trainers, owners, grooms and other riders, to watch the round on television. At each fence the mounted and ground stewards blow their whistles to alert the crowds to an approaching horse, and clear the course of spectators to give each rider a clear run at the obstacles. In the central control room the wooden blocks move silently along the Trotter board, and the master score sheets gradually fill up, recording the fate of each competitor.

In the competitors' tent there was admiring applause as Ginny Leng took the quick way through the centre of the Chevrons, the first of the difficult combination fences, and made it look simple. As she came up to the Lake, the tent was silent. Frank Weldon had made this a difficult combination, with a drop into the water and a fence on top of the jetty in the middle of the lake, which meant another drop before powering over the third element onto dry land. There were time-consuming alternatives that avoided the middle 'bounce', but the quick way was through the centre, and that was the route Night Cap was being steered towards. They dropped well into the water, trotted strongly at the jetty, neatly jumped up and over, but then on landing Ginny lost her reins and Night Cap slewed out to the left, missing the third element. The groans of disappointment from the thousands of spectators

Left: David Pease on The Politician at the New Moon, 1985.
Above: Tessa Martin Bird and The Mountaineer at the Quarry, 1981.

around the lake were echoed in the competitors' tent, for nowhere will you find a more fair-minded bunch of athletes than in eventing. But while Ginny collected unwelcome penalties for a refusal, her mistake was valuable to the watchers. Riders who had decided to take the easier routes were now confident that they had made the right decision, while those who had decided to follow her lead made a mental note to hold on tight after the second element, and steer like mad for the right-hand side. As Night Cap galloped over the line at the end of an otherwise faultless round, the electronic clock showed a total of time 13 min. 32 sec. just 1.20 over the optimum time. As 0.4 of a penalty point is added for every second over the optimum time of 12.12, that meant Night Cap was awarded 32 penalties, to be added to the 20 for the refusal at the Lake. While Ginny went through the necessary formalities of dismounting in front of the official BHS steward and weighing-in to make sure they were still carrying the minimum 11 stone 11 lb her score was being entered on the main computer and painted onto the master scoreboard at the head of the trade stands. The first rider was home and dry, every part of the machine had proved that it was well oiled and working, and would keep running for each of the fifty-two horses that were still to come. By lunchtime there was a steady two-way traffic of horses in and out of the stableyard. For some riders there was the elation of having got round, for others the disappointment of being eliminated or having to withdraw. Whatever the circumstances of the ride, the horses looked the same. Heads bowed with exhaustion, flanks shining and flecked with sweat. Although the wet going had not affected the jumps, it did make the gallops between the

*Top: Janice Yeo on Kinsfold at the
Stockholm Fence, 1986.
Left: Polly Schwerdt on Dylan II at the
Slide, 1984.
Right: Duncan Douglas on Mr. Twink,
1980.*

obstacles sticky and holding, and that drained the energy reserves of even the fittest horses. Each animal was slowly walked back to its stall, unsaddled, and then taken to the 'wet' room just off the main yard to be hosed down and cleaned of mud, perspiration and grease. Rugged and bandaged, and after the offer of a long, cool drink, each was given a bran mash and bulging hay net, and then left in peace to recover and rest. For some there were ice packs on bruises, poultices on sore legs, and anxious hands gently probing and feeling for bumps or undue heat in the joints. In contrast there were horses still waiting to go, shaking with anticipation, and prancing out of the yard for all the world as if they were off to do battle, like the nineteenth-century chargers they were emulating.

True to form, Weldon's course was sorting out the real championship material from the rest. Fence four, the Chevrons, was claiming its crop of victims, as were the Ski Jump and the Coffin, with a whole bunch of riders also falling foul of the Lake. In the competitors' tent the watchers rode every fence with their fellow equestrians, making encouraging 'clicking' noises or shouting 'Go on – gee up!' as if their combined vocal power alone would get horse and rider over each obstacle. As the afternoon went on the Red Cross were kept busy putting eleven stitches in the cut hand of one of the caterers and mending a spectator's broken arm. The police made two arrests for shoplifting, and in the main arena the boys of the Avon and Bristol Federation of Boys' Clubs were building the show jumping course, under the careful eye of course designer Alan Ball – not as spectacular, perhaps, as the jumps that were the centre of attention out in the Park, but still a vital element in deciding the ultimate winner.

Just before 3 o'clock David Green and Walkabout began their circuit of the steeplechase course. There were only four horses to go after him, so the officials were looking forward to packing up and possibly catching the tail end of some of the cross-country on television. At the judges' briefing the previous Sunday one of the stewards had told me how, in 1985, they had finished their day in a blinding snowstorm. On that occasion, too, David Green had been one of the last riders to go round, and just when they assumed their day was almost over David's horse, Shannagh, stumbled and fell, putting them out of the competition. 'It was quite a shock to the system having our one and only emergency right at the end of the day,' she had said. In 1986 Shannagh was ridden by David's wife, Lucinda Green, who had already gone through the steeplechase course half an hour before and was well on her way to the start of Phase D. David and his horse Walkabout were watched with extra care. The judges didn't want to be caught out a second year running! Walkabout made light work of the nine steeplechase fences, and the judges relaxed once he cleared the last, registering a time that was just seven seconds over the optimum. As the horse slowed back to a walk he suddenly stumbled, and fell. But he didn't get up. Walkabout was dead.

There was no need to stop the competition. The horse was well clear of the track, so as the last four horses completed Phase B Walkabout was loaded into the horse ambulance and taken off to the hunt kennels, where the duty vet could perform a post mortem. He was later to tell a still stunned rider that Walkabout had died of a heart attack, something described as 'one of those little time bombs that can go off at any time'. It was a tragic day for David, who later had the added horror of watching his wife, Lucinda, take one of the most spectacular falls ever seen at Badminton.

Mandy Jenkins comes to grief at The Lake on Woden, 1985, but at least she didn't get a ducking!

Coming into the Stockholm fence Shannagh took off too early, slid into the huge tree trunk and catapulted his rider over his head a good 12 feet into the air. In the competitors' tent there were shrieks as Lucinda made a dive, arms outstretched, down into the ditch on the landing side of the fence. There was stunned silence as the television cameras cut to a close-up of the top of the ditch, where there was no movement, every rider knowing that from a fall like that you would expect to break an arm at least, at worst your neck or back. Then a huge cheer went up as first Lucinda's hand, groping for her crop, and then her head appeared over the rim of the ditch. Then she emerged, covered in mud, and went straight to the horse to make sure he was sound. Someone shouted out, 'Trust Lucy to be more worried about the horse than herself!' but the nervous laughter showed how relieved everyone was. There were comments about the ditch being full of pig slurry from the farm, and Lucinda 'smelling pretty high', which as it turned out was true, but the soft mud had probably saved her neck – quite literally – so no one was complaining. A few fences later, at the Lake, Lucinda had the watchers on their feet again when she was unseated and clung on desperately to Shannagh's neck until he walked out of the penalty zone, where she could not be penalized for touching the ground, before remounting. Such is the mark of a truly brilliant rider, that even while hanging upside down and getting soaking in the lake, you can still work out the options that give you just 20 penalties for leaving the zone, as against 60 penalties for a fall inside it. On the main scoreboard the clear leader all afternoon was young Rachel Hunt, who had scorched around the course on Piglet II just seven seconds over the optimum time, and cannoned into first position from forty-seventh after the dressage.

With just one rider to go it looked as though the result was cut and dried. But then tail end Charlie Ian Stark and Sir Wattie rode a faultless round, one of only eleven clear rounds that day, and although they were slightly slower than Rachel, Ian's good dressage score meant he finished with 68.1 penalties and snatched the lead in the last moments of the second day.

In spite of the mud, and the rain that had marred the second half of the afternoon, the cars were cleared quickly off the grass car parks, where the tractors did sterling work. In the trade area shoppers were still milling around anxious to spend, and able to laugh as they walked, ankle deep, through pools of liquid mud. Let's face it, if we British did not have a sense of humour about our weather, we would never go anywhere!

In the stables there was a mixture of emotions. For some it had been a day of glorious achievement, regardless of whether they were going to win or not. For others, one of great disappointment. Many competitors were verbally reriding the course, analysing the mistakes they had made, wishing they had taken a different route, or animatedly reliving the excitement of it all, and to a man (and woman) praising their mounts as the cleverest, the bravest and the best. Soon the yard was echoing to the sound of horses being walked slowly around to help ease any stiffness after the afternoon's exertions. There was a special concern for Polly Schwerdt's brave little horse, Dylan II. At sixteen years old and 15 hands high he was the oldest and smallest horse in the championships, and a great favourite with Badminton regulars. On the gallop up to the second fence the horse had been hit by a stray car that ignored the steward's warning to clear the course. Dylan had galloped smack into the side of it, and by some miracle was not badly injured. He

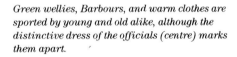

Green wellies, Barbours, and warm clothes are sported by young and old alike, although the distinctive dress of the officials (centre) marks them apart.

*Opposite page top: Karen Lenden (USA) on
March Brown at Lexington Dog Kennels, 1979.
Bottom: Mary Hunter and Bugsy Malone at the
Ski Jump, 1984.
This page top: Andy Brake on Bampton Fair at
the Luckington Lane in 1979.
Bottom: David Green on Walkabout II over the
Frauenfeld platform on his way into the
Quarry.*

David Green parts company with Mairangi Bay at the last element of the Bull Pens jump, 1983.
Right: Helen Ogden on Streetlighter at the Bullfinch, 1986.

had a small cut on the chest, and was pronounced fit to continue. Apart from one unfortunate stop three fences later at the Chevrons that game little horse had a brilliant round, but now there were fears that the bruises from the impact might make him too sore to continue the competition on Sunday. Later that evening the Schwerdts, and four other competitors with grievances, had their complaints heard by the ground jury. Four queries over penalty points were not upheld, but the jury agreed that Dylan had not only been stopped but penalized by the accident so they gave him a bonus of forty-five seconds to be deducted from the overall time on the speed and endurance section. Honour was satisfied, and all the family could do now was keep their fingers crossed that Dylan would be fit the following morning.

Throughout the evening the vets had a busy time checking and advising. But there were no serious problems, and most riders went to bed that night confident that their horses would trot up sound for the following morning's veterinary inspection. At one time, cross-country day nerves would have been blown away at the famous Badminton Ball on Saturday evening, held in Westonbirt Girls School. But as the competition got tougher and the competitors more professional in their approach, the Ball was seen as a waste of valuable energy and sleeping time, and was dropped. Event riders still like to party – but after a competition, rarely during one.

At 7 a.m. on Sunday morning Frank Weldon was examining the state of the car parks. Almost 200,000 people had flocked into Badminton the previous day, in spite of the weather, and their cars had ploughed deep mud furrows in the land. An hour

Top: Heavy rain can cause sticky situations in the caravan park.

Bottom: Elizabeth Purbrick and Felday Farmer after falling at the water in 1980. Although the horse was jammed over the fence, quick work by the stewards soon had him released and both horse and rider were none the worse for the fall.

later he took the unprecedented step of closing all the car parks and announcing that the final phase of the competition would continue, but the public would not be allowed into the Park with their cars. They could walk in if they liked, but their cars would have to stay outside as a further motorized onslaught could do irreparable damage to the land. Early morning bulletins on local and national radio carried the news, and the traffic police organized an emergency plan to park cars along the roads leading to the village for those spectators still determined to see the competition through. Weldon also decided that instead of dividing the show jumping into two sections, with the lower-placed riders jumping first and the top twenty horses going at 3 p.m., the competition would run straight through from 11 a.m. without a break.

Only thirty-four of the original sixty horses were presented to the vets and the ground jury at 10 o'clock. Apart from those who had withdrawn for various reasons on Thursday and Friday, eighteen horses had been withdrawn or eliminated in the speed and endurance test, while two horses who had completed the course in fine style – Electron, who had gone clear, and the American horse Strike A Light, who had fallen at the water – had sustained minor injuries that left them too lame to be presented. Sunday's inspection is a telling time. Saturday's ride is a gruelling test of any horse's fitness and strength, but in less than twenty-four hours they have to be ready to jump again. Admittedly the twelve show-jumps are not enormous, at 3 ft 11 in maximum, but with the inclusion of a double, a treble, a water jump and a wall, it is still no pushover, and it takes an exceptional horse to jump a good round after jumping its heart out the previous day.

Senior vet Frank Mahon is not a man to be fooled, and at the slightest hint of lameness he will fail a horse. 'The first test on Wednesday is far more important than the Sunday morning inspection,' he told me. 'If a horse is lame to start with there is no way anyone would ever allow it to go through and take on the rigours of the competition. But on Sunday morning I can be a little more lenient. No sensible rider will present a horse that's truly lame, and if they do it still gets spun, but sometimes they are a little stiff or sore after Saturday, and in that case jumping isn't likely to harm or injure the horse in any way, and I would pass it.' A few horses did, perhaps, look a little tired, but most were shining after hours of grooming and still looked fit to jump for their lives. Even Dylan looked fully recovered, and got an appreciative cheer when they announced 'Number sixty-two: passed'.

While public attention was focused at the front of the house, police sniffer dogs trained to find explosives were searching the area around the Royal Box in the main arena in what is now, sadly, a routine aspect of Royal security.

Weldon was making sure that the appropriate flags and national anthems were available in case one of the overseas competitors suddenly leaped into the lead, as happened when New Zealand's Mark Todd won in 1980, and that all the prizes of money, rosettes, spurs, saddle, assorted bowls, trophies and plaques, as well as the trophy itself, were all lined up and ready to make the prizegiving a streamlined operation. It is a point of honour with Weldon that Badminton's ceremony should be over quickly, efficiently and with dignity, having seen the 'awful mess they make of it at some internationals'.

Once the show jumping began, at 11 a.m., it seemed to be over in no time at all. There was no parade of competitors, no music from the Royal Marine Band. It was as if, after all the rain and the mud, everyone just wanted to get on with the competition and get a result as soon as possible. And by 1 o'clock it was all over. Ian Stark confirmed his lead with a winning show jumping round in the pouring rain, to collect the Whitbread trophy from HRH Princess Anne. Because the event had finished so early, most of the riders began packing up and leaving for home almost at once, while a few stayed to celebrate with champion Ian Stark as he was fêted by sponsors and owners, the press and officials. There was only one sour note during the day. Several hundred people did not realize that the afternoon's jumping had been cancelled, and walked miles from their cars in time for the usual 3 o'clock start only to find everyone packing up. Assurances from the box office that they would get their money back for seats booked in advance did little to calm some tempers.

The post mortems would go on for weeks in the press, in stableyards and homes all over the country. But at the end of the day the general view was summed up by Lorna Clarke, who said, 'Frank got it right . . . but then he usually does'.

Above: 1985. Aerial view of the main ring, dressage/show jumping area, some of the thousands of cars that flock to Badminton on cross country day.
Right: Ricenda Lord on Mulberry Wine at the Stockholm fence, 1986.

9

THE WINNER

It is every serious event rider's goal to compete at Badminton, every competitor's dream to win.

Ian Stark, by winning the 1986 championships on the ten-year-old Sir Wattie, is now one of that elite corps of riders who have realized both ambitions. For him the moment of truth, when he knew he had done it, came the second he landed over the final fence in the show jumping ring. He had had one fence down, but that did not matter. He was far enough in the lead to know the minute Sir Wattie's front legs landed clear over the wall that the championship was his. A huge grin split his face in two, his left arm punched the air in triumph, then went round the horse's neck in gratitude as he splattered through the mud of the collecting ring at full gallop to the tears and cheers of the Stark camp. Like most riders who have won this great competition, he admits that he went through the prizegiving ceremony in a 'bit of a daze' – receiving the trophy from the hands of Princess Anne, taking the lap of honour at full gallop, rosette ribbons flying, the photographs with the event sponsors, his own sponsors and owners, the parties, the champagne and the congratulations.

It was not until hours after the last glass had been drained, at 8.30 on a damp Monday morning, that the full impact of being a Badminton winner finally struck home. He was the last rider to leave the stables; we sat talking through the events of the previous week in the great servants' hall at Badminton House, surrounded by the silent stags' antlers, the wood smoke of a dying fire, and the memories of an outstanding five days. Sir Wattie's hooves echoed round the mellow stone

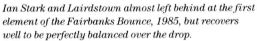

*Ian Stark and Lairdstown almost left behind at the first
element of the Fairbanks Bounce, 1985, but recovers
well to be perfectly balanced over the drop.*

Above: Preliminary vet check.
Right: David Stevensen, Ian Stark and Sir Wattie, 1986.

courtyard as he was led into the horsebox for the journey home to Scotland, while his rider came to terms with the reality of success. 'I was so excited yesterday – I knew I'd won it, but I think this morning it's really registered for the first time.' He is not the first, and certainly won't be the last rider to admit: 'It's been such a lifelong ambition to ride here, that to win it was way beyond any hopes. One dreams of it – and that's about it.' But when you can run your hands over the smooth lines of the silver Whitbread trophy, you know it is no longer a dream, and that the years of hard work and disappointments, the hopes and the gut-churning anxieties, have all been worth it. But how does that journey to the top begin?

When does a rider start preparing for Badminton? Is it six months before the event, when the autumn schedule for horse trials is well under way; a couple of years before, when the 'right' horse trots into the yard; or half a lifetime away, when the young rider gets his or her foot inside a stirrup for the first time?

Ian Stark has no hesitation in saying: 'It was always my ambition to ride here, from as long back as I can remember. Just watching it on television made it always the big aim of my life to get here.' So for him the ambition took root when he was ten or eleven years old in the mid 1960s. It was almost another twenty years before he realized the first part of the dream and actually competed at Badminton, which he did in 1984 with two horses, Oxford Blue (who finished third and subsequently went on to the Los Angeles Olympics, securing ninth individual place and helping the British team to clinch the silver medal), and Sir Wattie (who finished a creditable sixth in his first outing over Weldon's demanding Gloucestershire course).

In fact 1984 looked like being a great year for the young Scotsman. Only two years before he had been working in an office, riding and competing in every precious spare moment. In 1982 he took the plunge and gave up his clerical job to work full time in his own yard near Selkirk. And it was paying off. In two years he had qualified two horses for his first Badminton, both had been placed in the ribbons, and both had caught the eye of the Olympic selectors. The Edinburgh Woollen Mill stepped in just before the Olympics with valuable sponsorship, and both Dame Jean Maxwell-Scott and Susan Luczycwyhowska, who owned Sir Wattie, agreed to let Ian go on competing with the horse. So the immediate future was financially secure, and by the autumn he had a quarter share in an Olympic silver medal. But you do not have to work with horses for long to discover that just when everything is looking rosy fate is most likely to give you a kick in the pants. At the Burghley Horse Trials in the autumn of 1984 Sir Wattie confirmed just how much he hated jumping bullfinch fences by taking one badly and bruising a tendon. Ian knew that would put him out of work for the rest of the season, so he went to Badminton the following year with just one horse – his Olympic star, Oxford Blue. They parted company in the Quarry after a crashing fall, and returned to Scotland defeated, though still determined. For the rest of the year Sir Wattie quietly grazed in the fields at home while Ian notched up even more successes on the new arrival, Deansland, and won the team gold and individual silver medal in the European Championships riding Oxford Blue.

The start of the hunting season in Scotland hailed Sir Wattie's return to work. Ian admits, 'Normally I don't bring my horses into work until the beginning of January, but because he'd had a year off I wanted to make sure that his legs would stand up to the work.' His wife Jenny hunted Wattie regularly with the Duke of Buccleuch's until January, when he had a short break. The legs were sound, the horse was fit, and Badminton was just three months away. Ian was in no doubt that Wattie would run. 'He's always had a special air about him,' he says, 'He's a really tough horse, and although he needed that year's rest I never thought he would "go off" and not want to compete again. So if anything was going to go round Badminton I knew he would, and that became the goal.'

Getting the horse fit for the championships was no problem. The Stark yard is just on the eastern edge of the Tweedsmuir hills, so there is no need for the complex precision of interval training – 'just good old-fashioned hacking up and down the hills'. With an understanding of the special character of the horse ('He's a bit stuffy,' says Ian, 'and needs a lot of galloping'), and the broad sweep of the Southern Uplands on his doorstep, the flying Scotsman had all he needed to bring the horse up to peak condition.

Although Wattie was already qualified on points for Badminton from his previous run, he needed to complete at least one advanced competition in the spring to establish that qualification. So in early March they went off first to Aldon and then to Dynes Hall, with the final test at Brigstock, where they picked up an encouraging third place, just three weeks before the championships.

By now horse and rider were installed at Mark Todd's establishment near Andover. At the beginning of March Ian had loaded up Sir Wattie, Oxford Blue and his latest advanced horse, Glenburnie, for the seven-hour journey south. Oxford Blue was taken straight to Wylye, where he went into quarantine with the rest of the horses short-listed for the World Championships in Australia in May. Sir Wattie and Glenburnie settled down thirty miles away over the border in Hampshire, and Ian began the daily trek between the three horses, working them through a steady programme that he hoped would bring each animal to a peak at exactly the right moment.

At Wylye, like all the World Championships horses, Oxford Blue came under the meticulously critical eye of Lady Hugh Russell during his cross-country training, and both Sir Wattie and Glenburnie reaped the benefit of her skills, and those of the rest of the team trainers, in their own preparation for the three days of Badminton. As Ian points out: 'Until I was short-listed for Los Angeles I'd never had a cross-country or show jumping lesson in my life . . . so it was rather interesting to get some help!' Until then his mother-in-law, Jean McAulay, a former competitor herself, and now a dressage judge, had helped him considerably backed up by dressage coach Barbara Slane Flemming. But now, with the combined talents of Lady Hugh, Pat Burgess for show jumping and Ferdi Eilberg for dressage, Ian was able to soak up the expertise of some of the finest trainers in the world, and apply those skills to every one of his competition horses.

After Brigstock Wattie had a few days off, with just a little walking and trotting; Ian knew that two weeks steady work before the competition would be enough to bring the horse back to his peak fitness in time for the cross-country test at Badminton. The Hampshire landscape around Mark Todd's yard does not have the advantage of Ian's native Scottish hills, but the two riders exercised their horses together, and Ian was interested to discover that he and Mark have fairly similar training methods. These included not overworking the horses at dressage. Says Ian: 'When they reach the right standard for competitions like Badminton I don't feel they need a lot of dressage because they get bored with it. You just have to keep it fresh in their minds.' So for Wattie there was just a little work in the indoor school, but lots of hacking around the Hampshire lanes and galloping over the downs, 'which he loves'.

On the Tuesday before the competition the Starks were on the move again, this time for the comparatively short journey across country to Badminton. All morning the Badminton team were loading the lorry with equipment, including the kitchen sink, for this would be his 'home' for the duration of the competition. The team consisted of Ian's wife Jenny, her second cousin, Sandi Miller, over on holiday from Ireland, Claire Davis, who had been Ian's groom in Los Angeles and had taken a week's holiday from her secretarial job so as not to miss the fun, and head lad Ian Cootie. They packed away the saddles and bridles, bandages and rugs, food and first aid kit, spares of vital pieces of equipment. All the appropriate clothes for dressage, cross-country and show jumping were included, with spare breeches and shirts and so on. Each item was meticulously checked and double checked. There appeared to be enough equipment to service a small cavalry troop. And finally the horses, Sir Wattie and Glenburnie, rugged and bandaged, and each carrying his rider's hope of 'maybe third time lucky'.

They arrived at Badminton during the early evening, went through the formalities of presenting their passports to the official vet, and then 'checked in' to the stableyard. While the team unpacked what needed to be unpacked, prepared the horses' beds and evening feed, Ian took each of his mounts on a gentle trot around the Park to 'give them a chance to see everything and to get the feel of the place before the vet's inspection on the following day'.

On Wednesday morning Ian attended the riders' briefing with the rest of the competitors at 10 a.m. in the village hall. Having collected his map of the course, the official brochures and the rest of the necessary paperwork, he went off to work his horses, putting off his first look at the course until the following day.

Glenburnie had been drawn number 45 and Sir Wattie 89. This meant that both horses would ride their dressage tests on Friday, with Glenburnie the first to go at 9 a.m., and Wattie, the last horse in the competition, at 4.20 p.m. This gave Ian the whole of Thursday to work on the horses and to walk the course for the first time. The previous evening he had avoided talking in any detail to those riders who had already taken a look at Frank Weldon's new horrors, leaving his mind clear to make his own judgements.

On Thursday morning he walked the course – alone, preferring to trust his own opinion about each fence and how it should be jumped. Even before he started out past the first hurdle of the Whitbread Barrels he was anxious about the conditions, as it had rained solidly throughout the night. 'Badminton is always enormous. Every fence has to be attacked. It's a test for any horse on good going, but when you are coming out of six inches of mud, they've got to be exceptional horses.' After weeks of rain the mud was everywhere.

The first half of the course presented no major problems. As he ticked off the fences one by one he opted for the quick route every time; through the middle of the Chevrons, over the corners of Luckington Lane and the Vicarage Vee, over the log at the Stockholm Fence, and the drop at Horsen's Bridge. He had ridden this way round the course two years before on Sir Wattie, and with that experience had a good idea of how the horse would react to each of the obstacles.

He got to the Lake fence, number 18, before he was stopped in his tracks with a problem to solve. 'One drop into the water is quite difficult, but to have two, and then a third fence coming at you very quickly, is no picnic. But then the "easy" route was also very difficult, and such a long way round. So after I'd looked at it from every angle I decided that there was only one way to go, and that was straight through the middle – but I didn't think for one minute that it was going to be easy.' The second major problem loomed just two fences later, at the Ski Jump. When he saw it first he reckoned: 'In the sticky going they could come over the log at the top and just slide all the way down to the rail at the bottom, and then turn over.' But a closer inspection convinced him that 'they might just about keep their feet, and take off from the bank. It's not quite as steep as the Hickstead Bank, but I wouldn't think that the show jumpers would fancy tackling it and having to take off half way down. Certainly, seeing the fence for the first time, I thought it was almost unfair in the conditions.' The rest of the course presented no major problems, with Ian deciding on the quick way through the Coffin, and expecting a problem at the next fence, the big Bullfinch at the bottom of the hill, remembering what had happened with Wattie eighteen months before at Burghley.

He went back to the stables to start working the two horses, sloshing through the mud, and knowing that apart from the two problem fences his biggest worry

Right: Ian Stark and Sir Wattie riding their dressage test in 1986.

was whether or not to run the young horse Glenburnie as the ground became steadily worse. An eight-year-old grey gelding, Glenburnie is clearly very special to Ian. 'Without running down any of my other horses, I think he's the best horse I've ever ridden. I was very keen to bring him because I think he's terrific, what I reckon is my star of the future. So there's no point in giving him a big fright this early on.' Sir Wattie presented no such problems. 'He's always had that special air about him,' says Ian, 'and I knew that if anything would go round in the mud, he would.'

While the first thirty horses went through their paces in the dressage arena on Thursday, Ian Stark got on with working his horses in preparation for their own tests on Friday. Watching the gathering rain clouds, he knew that whatever happened to the weather on Friday night would decide whether he rode two horses or just one over Saturday's thirty-two championship fences.

On Thursday night the heavens opened, and in the main ring on Friday morning the dressage arena bore the scars of the previous day's competition where the horses had cut a muddy track in a pattern of loops and diagonals. Glenburnie was first to go at 9 a.m., when the stands were practically deserted, and although Ian had felt that 'his dressage wouldn't be top of the tree here', he was pleasantly surprised. 'Normally when you go into a dressage arena at Badminton the tension is so great that you lose a lot of the horse's concentration, which is what I expected to happen with Glen . . . but he was quite the opposite. In fact, he's never gone better.' This feeling was reflected in the young horse's score of 55, which put them in tenth place overall. Clearly Glenburnie was living up to his 'star' qualities!

Wattie was rather a different proposition. 'He can always do a good test when he's calm and relaxed, but he can get very tense if the atmosphere gets to him. Then his whole body shortens and the knees come up and nearly hit his chin . . . and you get terrible marks.' So Wattie's preparation for the test was hardly the conventional calm, steady approach favoured by most dressage riders. Instead, Ian took him off for a long hack of an hour and a half around the roads and tracks of the estate 'just to get him relaxed away from the tension of the actual competition'. To round off the morning he galloped the horse along the perimeter of the Badminton airstrip next to the steeplechase course, and then put him back in his stable for a couple of hours, while Ian went off for another look at the cross-country fences.

His test was at 4.20 p.m. Forty-five minutes before he swung up into the saddle and calmly walked through the crowds at the rear of the trade stands. He worked quietly for a few minutes in the warm-up area to the side of the collecting ring and then went straight through to perform the test. By now the tapestry of the dressage test was clearly etched in a series of muddy paths. Fortunately Wattie does not mind the mud. As Ian puts it, 'We were rather chuffed' at their mark of 46.80, which gave them a comfortable third place at the end of the first day.

While the grooms fed and fussed over the two horses Ian went back for another look at the course. Although it had not rained at all during the day he was still terribly worried. 'Not just for the young horse, but also for Wattie. I thought that because the ground conditions were so bad the competition was going to be very difficult for the majority of horses.' So as he walked the four and a half miles of the course for the third time his mind was full of the problems being set not just by the course builder but also by the Almighty. 'I was worried in general because jumping out of sticky, holding mud will tire horses, and possibly frighten horses, so there could be a lot of falls. If that happened then it wouldn't do the horses' or the riders' confidence any good, and it certainly wouldn't do the reputation of the sport any good. But admittedly by the end of Friday night I did think that things were looking a bit better. The ground had been drying out all day, and provided that it didn't rain overnight, then it wasn't going to be too bad. And I got back to the stable all set to run both horses next day.'

But it did rain overnight. Not an eight-hour downpour, but enough to undo all the good of the previous day's drying wind. At 8.30 a.m. Ian was out on the course once more, walking each yard meticulously and re-examining his options at some of the fences. Even at that early hour Ian, and the dozen or so like-minded riders who were also out having one last look, were not alone. 'It was incredible. There were hundreds of spectators out walking the course.' I can understand his incredulity. The previous day I had watched the great British public walking in their hundreds along the very line that the horses would be taking on cross-country day. The non-stop procession of wellie-booted feet laid a neat snail's trail of mud from one fence to the next. Like most of the riders, Ian did not exactly appreciate this aspect of the public's interest in the horse trials. 'They've paid money to get in, and they're entitled just as much as we are, but when the ground is so bad I think it would have been better to keep them off the actual course, and have them walking on the outside of the boundary ropes. I know Colonel Frank's idea is that the general public act as a steamroller and pack the ground down, but with all that rain it meant that the takeoffs and landings were all poached and chewed up. No grass at all, just mud. It had got wetter, and stickier, so I went straight back and pulled my young horse out.'

He also rethought his tactics on two of the fences for Wattie. At the Chevrons, where he had originally decided to go straight through the middle, he looked more seriously at the right-hand alternative, taking the first element on an angle, with a bounce between it and the second pole, then two strides out on the left-hand side of the fence close to the inn sign. The Ski Jump was not so straightforward. 'I looked at the possibility of riding off the slope to the right and then jumping the fence at the bottom from the left. But I finally felt it would have been impossible to do that with the slippery conditions . . . the horse's legs would just have skidded on the bank, so I kept to the original plan.' As last man to go he was not due to start out on Phase A, the first section of road and tracks, until 2.56 p.m., which meant he could watch at least half the field tackling the cross-country course before even getting into the saddle. He did not bother to go up to the steeplechase course. He had ridden Wattie alongside the course the previous morning, and felt that the going had been good. Instead he went straight to the competitors' tent in the middle of the starting box, where two television screens monitored the progress of the cross-country riders. His reaction to what he saw was horror. 'Of the first nine horses that went round there wasn't one that didn't have a problem somewhere. Even Night Cap was finding it difficult. Not just at the Lake, but coming into the Stockholm Fence as well. He was worried for such an experienced horse, and at that point I knew I was right to have pulled out my young horse.' That salutary hour or so in the box also confirmed that he was right to take the alternative he had seen at the Chevrons. 'I'd seen so many people who opted for the middle route just running out down the leg instead, that I decided it wasn't worth the risk.' With fifteen minutes to spare Ian was in the starting box for Phase A. A small, almost lonely group of just horse, rider, grooms and well-wishers, with the officials counting down the seconds to the off at precisely 2.56 p.m. By now the great huddle of spectators had gone off to watch the excitement on the cross-country course, so few people witnessed the start of what was to be a championship run.

Phase A was a steady, uneventful hack. On the steeplechase course Wattie had to do the first serious work of the day. The going had turned to 'holding' and was tiring a lot of the horses even before they got to the cross-country phase, so Ian knew he would have to ride the horse with extra care, especially as he is 'pretty hard going on the 'chase at the best of times – he doesn't like to go that speed naturally, he would rather go a gear slower, but to do the course in the time you have to keep working.' In fact they were two seconds over the allotted time of four and a half minutes, and Ian says: 'He did actually try quite hard, but he was more tired than normal after the 'chase. He pulled up and put his head down as if to say "thank heavens that's over". He was just a bit puffed so I gave him about half a mile just walking at the start of the next phase, but then he started trotting again and perked up very quickly.'

At the end of Phase C, the final part of the roads and tracks, the riders come back into the Park at Badminton down the long Worcester Avenue and past the fences on the northern edge of the course. After the solitary ride through the estate's woodlands it is something of a shock suddenly to find yourself surrounded by some of the 200,000 people watching the all-important Phase D. But according to Ian it creates just the right sort of atmosphere for the horses. 'In spite of the mounted stewards shouting and screaming at people to get out of the way, so that we can have a clear run to the starting box, they still seem to stand around. But it does perk the horses up again; they seem to get quite cheerful getting back into the atmosphere and the crowds.'

In the starting box Ian's team were ready to start greasing Wattie's legs to help them slide over the obstacles, walking him round, loosening the girth – all the pampering and preparation that is needed in that official ten-minute halt to prepare him for the next, most gruelling stage of the competition.

While Wattie was surrounded by his team, Ian was being administered to by another team – the invaluable advisers and watchers who can bring a rider up to date on what has been happening on the cross-country course while he has been out of touch riding the earlier phases.

Ian's team were a couple of fellow riders, Robert Lemieux and Clarissa Strachan, and his trainer Barbara Slane Flemming. As he says, their support was invaluable. 'I knew there had been so many problems at the start of the day, and so I needed to get into the right frame of mind. I knew Lucinda had had two falls, and that David Green's horse had collapsed on the steeplechase course, so I was getting more and more worried by the second. But they were all just marvellous. Robert and Clissie went over each fence with me and told me exactly what trouble there had been, where and why. They said: "Think again if you're worried about a particular route. Get out there . . . get your act together, and do a good job." It was just what I needed.' And whatever that pep talk did to his adrenalin, it certainly worked. It was almost a textbook ride, recorded in the mind, to be recalled and reridden stride by stride.

'Over the first half of the course he was brilliant, and bombing on quite a lot faster than I'd intended to go in that mud. But he felt so good I thought, "I'm not

The 1986 champions, Ian Stark on Sir Wattie and the victory gallop (below).

going to restrict you, because you're probably going to get tired when we get to the end of the course," so I let him go at his own speed. I took the alternative route at the Chevrons, and that was so neat we didn't really lose any time at all. The only slight hiccup was at the Vicarage Vee: going over the corner one of his back legs slipped into the ditch, and he hit the rail hard. But on the rest of the first half he was outstanding. At Horsen's Bridge I was a bit nervous, because two years ago when he competed here he hadn't jumped out far enough, he went over the rails and straight down. He was on his nose, and I was on his tail somewhere – we really hit it badly. So I rode into that one really strong, and he jumped it beautifully.

'From Horsen's up to the Drays it was really heavy going, and he started to make hard work of it. So after the Drays I had to give him a bit of a reminder. I did actually give him a bit of a smack with the stick, saying "get your act together, boy", and after that he came down towards the Lake really well. If anything he took me a bit close to the rails going in, and went straight down into the water. Then he trotted . . . it was a nightmare. I was expecting him to walk. Then he put in a short stride at the Jetty, which wasn't meant to happen, and caught a front leg on the top, which slightly tipped him forward going into the next [the Boathouse]. But he's so clever, I knew he would get away with it. I lost my reins and my stirrups, so we were coming into the third element totally out of control. I just kicked and flapped. I was lucky we were aimed in the right direction. It was terrible, I was doing absolutely nothing to help, but he's so confident it was as if he was saying "It's okay, we'll do it, just sit still," and he never touched it. Somehow, we were still intact, though Wattie was beginning to say, "This is hard work". Next was the Normandy Bank, and two years ago we had trouble there as well. But he's older and that much more experienced now, and jumped it well this year. Then it was on to the Ski Jump, which was worrying me so much. He came round the corner and never even looked at the log at the top of the slope. He just went straight over, half slipped on the slope, took two strides, and popped off over the rail at the bottom beautifully. I was so relieved, I reckoned that from then on – apart from the Coffin, which had caused more trouble than I ever thought it would – the course began to get a bit easier, so I though most of my trouble was over.'

The Coffin was in fact proving something of a bogey. Ten competitors picked up faults there, including the rider who was thundering round in front of Ian, Olympic champion Mark Todd. But Wattie went without mishap. He trotted two strides before the first element and caught a back leg on the rail as he landed, but this just checked him going through the middle, making the stride out perfect for him. As Ian says, 'It wasn't planned that way, but it worked for us.'

There was still a bit of a question mark over the next fence, the Bullfinch, but Wattie did not even pause. He just sailed through, and began the long pull uphill towards the Quarry. By now Wattie was feeling the effort of the ride, and Ian could feel the heart going out of his bold horse. 'He was really saying, "Please let me stop, I'm very tired".' But Ian couldn't give up now, and explains: 'It sounds a bit hard, but you have to say, "Come on, you must keep going, we're almost home, and it's all downhill".'

There is a unique bond between horse and rider that no other sportsman can ever experience. Success depends on the trust each has in the other's skill and courage. So Ian realized that for the last six fences on the course he would have to do more than just ride Wattie, he would have to nurse, cajole, persuade and will the big horse over every obstacle.

They jumped well into the Quarry, but the horse lost some of his impulsion in the bottom and it took every ounce of energy to get over the wall at the top of the bank. When he landed Wattie almost came to a standstill, but then he found a reserve of energy, bounded off and did not even check for the crossed poles over the yawning ditch of fence 28, the Cross Question. They went straight through the extraordinary-looking Huntsman's Hangover, and then they were just three fences from home. Wattie obviously recognized the run in and Ian felt him perk up. 'He jumped the last three fences beautifully, and that was such a relief because when I got to the Quarry I'd had serious doubts about whether or not he would be able to finish. But he's such an honest horse. He didn't fumble or scramble over fences as some horses do when they're tired. He's so good that every time we came to a fence he just said "Oh, another one", and got on with the job and cleared it.'

Not to put too fine a point on it, when Ian dismounted and was led off by Hugh Thomas to be interviewed by the BBC, he was 'overcome with emotion, and chuffed to bits'. It was during that live interview than Ian realized for the first time that he hadn't just gone clear, he'd gone into the lead. After the euphoria of that adrenalin-pumping ride came the reality that there was still one more phase of the competition to go. As Wattie had picked up 20.4 time penalties on the second day, this gave him an overall score, with dressage, of 68.00. Young Rachel Hunt had scorched round the course on Piglet II in the fastest time of the day, and was tucked in behind Ian in second place just 9.60 points behind. This meant that Ian could have one fence down in the show jumping, losing 5 penalty points, and still clinch the title. But two fences would cost him the championships.

Overnight Wattie had shrugged off the inevitable tiredness of the previous day's trial through the mud, and came out for the final vet's inspection on Sunday morning full of beans and raring to go. By tradition at Badminton for the show-jumping phase the riders compete in reverse order of their position at the end of the cross-country phase, not in numerical order as they do for the rest of the competition. Riders placed below twenty in the list jump before lunch on the Sunday, with the main part of the competition beginning at 3 p.m. But because on this occasion the weather had been so appalling that Frank Weldon had decided to run the show jumping competition straight through, the riders at the top of the list no longer had a leisurely day in front of them and there was a mad scramble to get into the show jumping ring to walk the course before 11 o'clock.

As Sir Wattie had not been brought before the vets until almost 10.45 a.m. there was not much time. Ian shot off to the main ring, and got there with two minutes to spare. He says: 'I *ran* round the course, I didn't walk it, and I was still looking at the last fence when the first rider came in to jump.'

He stood in the collecting ring to watch the first horses ride the course. He was especially keen to watch them through the treble. 'It's usually a big combination, with tight distances, but it had walked really rather well ... quite small ... so I thought that there had to be a trick there somewhere.' The first two horses crashed through the course, taking out thirteen fences between them. Ian could not bear to go on watching, so he went to get Wattie ready. He wanted to be back in the collecting ring, ready to jump, when there were about six to go before him. That way the horse would not get bored standing around, and he would not get too nervous. But his timetable went awry, and when he trotted into the enclosure there

Above: Princess Anne presents the Badminton trophy to Ian Stark.
Right: Ian Stark and Sir Wattie with the Whitbread trophy.

were still sixteen horses waiting to jump. The time dragged by, 'I was sitting on Wattie watching the competition. He started shivering, and at first I thought he was cold, but it was just excitement. Then I started shivering with the cold, and my stomach was in a knot. I could hardly bear to watch everyone else. It was just a nightmare. So I took him off to jump a few practice jumps. We put him over four fences, and he jumped them well, so I left it at that.'

With just two riders to go, the heavens opened and a furious rainstorm lashed the arena. Rachael Hunt had a fence down, which now gave Ian two fences in hand. But as he cantered across the arena he began to have serious doubts about his chances. The rain was so intense that he could not see the Royal Box, and his eyes were half shut against the rain trying to see where he was going through the downpour. In fact Wattie jumped well in the mud, even through the tricky treble, and such was Ian's level of concentration that he did not realize he had knocked the pole off the third fence. He came into the last thinking he was well in the clear, and admits: 'I nearly kicked for a very long stride because I thought that it really didn't matter. Then, when I landed clear and heard the announcer say "five penalties" I just couldn't believe it.'

But the extra five penalties did not matter. Wattie had won. He had shown style in the dressage arena, survived the mud and the gruelling test of the cross-country course, and come out full of running on the final day. As a lasting, tangible memorial, the names of Ian Stark and Sir Wattie will be entered on the Badminton Winners List. In more personal terms, Sir Wattie proved what Ian always knew, that he is a star, while for the rider himself there is the heady satisfaction of knowing that he has achieved a lifelong ambition – he has won at Badminton, a distinction that will remain, for so many in his sport, an impossible elusive dream.

10

HIGHLIGHTS

Every year, towards the back of the Badminton programme, somewhere between the advertisements and the list of trade stands, is the Roll of Honour – a list of all past winners of the competition. But this is much more than just a record of individual achievement, it is also a catalogue of excellence recalling Britain's progression from a country with virtually no competitive background in eventing to one that has produced more Olympic world and European champions than any other. In the thirty-seven years of the event's history more than 1700 horses and riders have competed at Badminton. To win the title just once has been the burning ambition of most of them, and each year it gets more and more difficult, with increasingly demanding fences and growing numbers of competitors, each one tougher, fitter, and more 'professionally' trained than before. To win just once is hard enough; to win more than once clearly takes a good deal more than the often quoted, though fickle and intangible extra ingredient, luck. It really is almost the logical conclusion of good preparation and gritty determination applied to a combination of horse and rider who both get it just right on the day.

Only five riders have ever managed to win more than once. Frank Weldon took the title in 1955, when the competition was held at Windsor, and again the following year when it returned to Gloucestershire. Olympic horseman Richard Meade has also made the double, with wins in 1970 on his European Championships horse The Poacher, and again in 1982 on Speculator III. Sheila Willcox has a unique three consecutive wins to her name, while Mark Phillips has taken the trophy four times and Lucinda Green lays claim to a remarkable record of six wins.

If you add to the list of winners the names that are engraved on the Armada dishes – the silver tokens that record five completed rounds at Badminton – you have a truly remarkable record of horsemen and women who collectively

*Right: Lorna Clarke on skewbald
Popadom, the most distinctive of the three
horses she rode in the 1970 competition,
jumping into the Lake.
Below: Captain Mark Phillips and
Columbus at the sunken foothpath, 1979.*

represent the skill and spirit that give eventing its unique sporting atmosphere.

It's a mark of Badminton's severity that many of Britain's finest and most famous riders have never actually won the coveted Badminton championships. Bertie Hill, for instance, a teammate of Laurence Rook at the 1956 Olympics in Stockholm, was still competing in 1970 – a year in which ten riders trained by him were also in the competition. Another determined rider who has never quite grasped the title is Lorna Clarke, who has ridden at Badminton a record-breaking sixteen times and became the first woman rider and only the second in the history of the event, to ride three horses in one competition. The closest she ever came to winning was finishing fourth in 1984. So while she's twice been a winner at Britain's other prestigious three day event, Burghley, and is also an Olympic, European and World Championship medallist, with an outstanding record worldwide in equestrian events, the Badminton trophy has always eluded her. She does, however, possess three Armada Dishes, one for every five completed competitions, and sums up, what for many is the whole spirit of Badminton when she says 'O.K. so they're just little silver ashtrays. But they're worth their weight in gold – plainly and simply because we risk our necks for them'. Another very successful rider – and one who competes under special pressures – is Princess Anne. Her first attempt on the championship was in 1971, riding Doublet, and on arriving in the stable yard for the first time she admits to wondering 'what on earth I am doing here?'. In fact her whole introduction to eventing was more by good luck than design. As she told me, 'I might have played polo, or given up riding altogether and done something completely different. But Col John Miller (The Queen's Equerry) gave me one of the horses he'd bred called Purple Star and I went to Alison Oliver to train. I found the combination of dressage, jumping and the cross country was so much more interesting and the little horse was quite entertaining, so we went on from there. It was a very humble beginning, and I hadn't planned it at all.'

As it turned out Purple Star wasn't suited to major competitions, so along came Doublet. As Princess Anne describes him he was 'an overgrown polo pony really, with no pedigree for the job. But we took it bit by bit and found that he enjoyed his work, and was on your side. We just followed a natural progression. Everything we asked him to do he did well. So Alison started thinking about Badminton. I don't think it would ever have crossed MY mind, but ignorance is bliss in youth, so I said "Oh alright".'

For any rider, competing in their first Badminton is nerve racking enough in itself. But for Princess Anne there was the added distraction of hoardes of press photographers. Press Officer Jim Gillmore confirms that in 1971 the numbers almost doubled, and they were all busily clicking away at every picture opportunity. If you've ever seen the Royal Watchers at work, you'll know that it's not a pretty sight, but Princess Anne clearly accepts their presence as par for the course. She says 'Everyone always thinks that it's going to make life difficult for me, but fortunately, to a large extent, I can close down mentally, concentrate on the horse and my trainer, concentrate on remembering the test and doing it right, and that did distract me from the other pressures.'

Dressage has never been a problem for Princess Anne, it's one of the equestrian disciplines she genuinely enjoys, and although at a one day event with an audience of one man and a dog, Doublet would perform – to quote his rider 'like an arthritic goat', with an audience he came alive and 'really sparkled'. So at his first

Top: Richard Meade on Speculator at the Whitbread barrels, 1982.
Right: Princess Anne on Goodwill.

Badminton, with the stands full and the arena crackling with anticipation, Doublet rode a fluid test, and finished in second place. When walking the cross-country course and being faced by Weldon's fences for the first time she remembers being 'numb, without any conception of what was about to happen' and so set off to ride the course on Saturday with the workmanlike attitude of just getting around clear and safe. In retrospect she says she 'enjoyed the ride enormously, mainly because I was so surprised to get any further than the second fence and the Coffin, which was number three, that I felt I had some chance of getting round the rest of the course'. The going that year was very wet, and the Princess remembers Doublet 'not making a tremendously good job of the Vicarage V, and not liking the Bullfinch in front of the Luckington Lane – but neither did I – and he took a hard look at the Elephant Trap. I wasn't over confident at the Normandy Bank because Doublet wasn't a great one for taking bounding leaps at things and letting fly. He was very inclined to put in a short one where he thought it necessary. So I really set off at the top of the hill towards that one, and he jumped it perfectly well, which was a comfort. The further we went the better he got. I just let him tick over at his own speed and he seemed to enjoy himself. I thought that to get round in one piece was actually an achievement, so I was quite pleased about finishing.'

In the show jumping ring Doublet put a foot in the water, so the combination picked up ten penalties and finished the three days in fifth place. But his rider wasn't disappointed. 'Considering he had never done a three day event, and I had only ridden in one, I think it was rather remarkable' is how she sums up that year, which was crowned by the combination winning the European championship in the autumn at Burghley.

Princess Anne has subsequently ridden at Badminton on four other occasions, each time on Her Majesty the Queen's horse Goodwill. The Princess had enormous respect and affection for the big brown horse. She says 'His jumping was so smooth and powerful, he was always a horse you felt could jump anything from anywhere. He soaked up the drop fences as though they didn't exist, but his dressage was a joke really. He was quite civilized about it, but the whole thing was agony to him, because he always felt under pressure'.

They came eighth in 1973 and fourth in 1974, the highest placing Princess Anne has ever achieved at Badminton. Since 1979 the Princess has never competed over the major three day course. Not that she wouldn't like to, but as one of the busiest members of the Royal Family she simply doesn't have the amount of time it would take to work herself, and a horse, into peak condition to make a serious attempt at the championship. Though she does still go whenever possible as a spectator, and like Lorna Clarke, regrets the loss of some of Badminton's old atmosphere. As she says 'The social side of the event used to be much more important, but sadly, it's all become much more "professional" in the sense that the riders can't spare the time. I think that's a shame because one of the pleasures of the three day event as opposed to the one day event, is the fact that you are all in the same place for four

Top right: Sheila Willcox with her famous horse High and Mighty, riding the dressage in 1957.
Centre right: Sheila Willcox receives the Badminton trophy for the first time in 1957.
Bottom right: Sheila Willcox and High and Mighty proved a winning combination again in 1958.

Above and right: Richard Walker on Accumulator in 1984.

or five days, and can share the experience with other competitors. So it seems a pity not to use that opportunity to get to know them better.'

She's enormously proud of the Armada dish she was awarded in 1980 for completing the course five times, and although the Whitbread Trophy will probably never bear her name, she has no regrets. Badminton has provided five major milestones in her equestrian career, so she can say without hesitation 'If I had to give it all up tomorrow, I'd be perfectly happy'.

Because so few record books ever bother to record who came second or third in the competition, the list of Badminton winners in the programme gives no clue to the fact that in 1959 the event was almost won by a member of 'Masters' own family – the man destined to become the present Duke of Beaufort, David Somerset.

It would certainly have been a particularly pleasing and fitting win, considering the enormous influence that Master had on the sport, but it wasn't to be. David Somerset, riding that great Olympic horse Countryman was pipped at the post on the last day by Sheila Willcox taking her third consecutive title.

You wouldn't expect him to be anything less than bitterly disappointed at his defeat, but with a true sportsman's generosity he says, 'Of course I would have loved to win such an exciting thing. But I always knew I was very much an amateur

compared with the others. Sheila was a proper rider, so I felt very lucky to have done as well as I did.'

Sheila Willcox is the only person ever to win the competition three years running – in 1957 and 1958 on High and Mighty, and again in 1959 under her married name of Sheila Waddington on Airs and Graces. In 1964 she won the Little Badminton event on Glenamoy.

The young Sheila Willcox was the archetypal 'horse mad teenager'. She lived in Lancashire, in an area where there was no hunting but lots of Pony Club activity and show jumping. It was a neighbour, Margaret Hough (winner at Badminton in 1954 on Bambi V) who told her about Badminton, and once she was hooked on the idea there was no doubt at all in her mind that one day she would win. With admirable candour she admits, 'While many people say taking part is enough, that's not for me. I've never been interested in coming second.' It is easy to see how she had all the guts and determination from which champions are made when she goes on to describe her attitude to competitive riding. 'As far as I'm concerned, if I had put in all the right work, done my preparation and everything that I should have done, then I shouldn't be beaten – unless, of course, there was an accident. But apart from that, it didn't enter my mind that I would be beaten.' She did all her own training, reading everything she could about getting horses fit, and then working to a meticulous eighteen-week fitness plan. Local horse shows gave her show jumping experience, dressage was a daily routine of work, putting into practice everything she could glean from books, from picking other people's brains, and watching riders in action. As there was no hunting locally she jumped her horses over everything she could find. 'On the nearby beach I'd jump overturned boats, stone walls – really nothing was safe from me.'

She was nineteen when she rode her first Badminton in 1965, and came second to Frank Weldon after a nail-biting finish, with just 1.56 points between them and what Sheila describes as 'a little hiccup on the cross-country with Kilbarry', when there was a question about whether or not the horse had stepped back at one of the fences. The young Miss Willcox had shown style and nerve, and she proved herself undisputed champion in the following three years, each time taking the lead after the dressage on day one, and staying ahead of the field for the rest of the competition. Her key word was, and still is, 'professionalism'. 'I've always had a thoroughly professional attitude to everything I've done,' she says. 'Those cross-country fences in my day weren't as technical as they are now, but they were big. They demanded enormous respect, and then, as now, Badminton was more intimidating than any other competition in the world.'

The youngest rider ever to win Badminton is Richard Walker, who took the title in 1969 when he was just eighteen. His 14-year-old horse, Pasha, at 15.1½ hands, was one of the smallest and oldest horses in the competition. The year before they had won the Junior European Championships, but with Olympic horses like Barberry, Cornisham V and The Poacher in the running, they were hardly hot favourites for the title at the start of the three days.

In such company, and in such a place, one might have expected the young rider to be overawed, but no. As Richard Walker tells it, 'I felt relatively confident in myself, and I had a very confident horse, so I was in the fortunate position of not having anything to lose. That's a very easy position to be in, and when you are totally wholehearted about something like that, and you have the combination of a pair of confident characters, the gamble can so easily come off.' His attitude is strikingly similar to that of Sheila Willcox, approaching the whole thing with a professional frame of mind, and there's the echo of her own dogma when he says, 'Bearing in mind our record in the Junior European Championships, I always hoped to do better than just get round. I think that deep down, if you are confident in your ability and preparation there's no reason why you shouldn't beat everyone else.'

Pasha was certainly not the easiest of horses to ride. He had a tendency to run away with his rider, and Richard was always 'slightly in trepidation about my capacity to hold him and guide him in exactly the right direction'. Lars Sederholm, Richard's trainer, is more direct. 'He was a little brute,' he says, 'a very difficult horse. It would take two of us to hold him at the start of Phase A [the roads and tracks], and once he was off he would just run away at his own speed. He never looked as though he was out of control because Richard always rode him with such beautiful balance, but I don't think he could ever have gone much slower.' There is one outstanding moment from that competition that proved to the spectators not only what a very fine rider Richard Walker was (and is), but also that Pasha was a horse determined to 'do his own thing'. In Huntsman's Close there was a set of posts and rails after a drop fence. The rails were arranged as two separate fences at 3 ft 6 in on the left and 3 ft 10 in on the right, separated by a high deer park fence, which was not to be jumped. On landing over the drop the rider had to turn either left or right, weaving slightly through a clump of small pine trees to get a clear approach to either of the two obstacles. Pasha had other ideas. As they landed over the drop Richard had intended to turn right-handed through the trees to take the higher of the two post and rail fences. But flying over the previous fence Pasha had already seen his way out – straight ahead and over the deer fence, which stood at about 4 ft 9 in high. He ignored his rider completely and just kept going. Says Richard, 'My heart was pumping so fast I just couldn't believe what was happening. He broke through the top rail, I lost both stirrups and was almost out the side door. But we managed to stay together, and got over the next fence, the Elephant Trap, which came up very suddenly. It took him at least the next five fences to get over it and he was very difficult to hold, but then he settled.'

At the end of the day Richard went back to look at the fence, 'because I still couldn't believe that we'd survived it', and although the route was unorthodox it counted, because he had cleared the obstacle between the red and white marker flags. By the end of Saturday Richard Walker and Pasha were in the lead. A clear show jumping round on the final day clinched the title, and later that year the combination went on to ride in the team that took European honours at Punchestown in Ireland.

It was almost inevitable that Mark Phillips would have a close association with Badminton. His parents, keen hunting folk, first took him to the event even before he could walk. It became a regular outing in the family calendar, and he still has vivid impressions as a very small boy of seeing Anneli Drummond-Hay jumping a zigzag, roughly where the Normandy Bank is now, on Merely-a-Monarch, and watching Australian rider Laurie Morgan take what to his young eyes was a 'ridiculously unjumpable' fence on Salad Days in 1960, the year he went on to win the team gold at the Rome Olympics. At about the same time Mark was receiving instruction from Frank Weldon as a member of the Beaufort Hunt Pony Club, and as he says, 'Because we lived at Great Somerford, so very close to Badminton, as children the competition was the biggest local happening of the year. We grew up almost in the shadow of it, so there was never an individual moment or day when I decided I would enter, it was simply always an ambition to ride the course.'

At his first attempt in 1968 Officer Cadet Phillips (as he then was) finished fourth on Rock On. He found the experience exhilarating. Three years later he was back again, this time with Great Ovation. 1971 had no reason to look promising. The previous autumn the horse had buried him over the course at Boekelo in Holland. As he says, 'It was very much a case of being here for the beer, and although we were in the lead at the end of the dressage I still wasn't absolutely sure about him across country and I set off just with the intention of getting round.' That year, luck – in the guise of someone else's misfortune – really did play a part in the result, as Mark himself admits. 'An Irish horse had got stuck on the Normandy Bank just ahead of me, so I was held up half way round the course. It meant we were hanging around for almost twenty minutes, so when I was given the "Go" it was like starting again on a fresh horse. During that stop I had time to realize that although it was very wet and slippery, he hadn't gone so bad, and what I had to ride on the second half of the course was no more than I'd do at a one-day event. So when we got going I set off with a very different attitude of mind. I had a fresh horse, and my foot was really down on the accelerator, to go as fast as I could from then on.' The slow, careful ride round the first half of the course meant that he still picked up some time penalties, but he finished clear, with the fourth fastest time of the day, maintaining a lead that was confirmed with a flawless show jumping round on the final day and a perfect winning finish.

Being handed the silver Whitbread Trophy by Her Majesty the Queen was, as he recalls, 'The best moment of my sporting life, only equalled by having the gold medal put round my neck in Munich the year after. But this was the realization of an ambition – I couldn't believe it. And although I look back now and laugh, I remember being so chuffed because I had to go to the sponsors' tent and answer questions for the press. People were asking me for my autograph, and Dorian Williams interviewed me on telly. Nobody had ever wanted to talk to me before, and suddenly I had arrived.'

The following year Mark made it a double, winning on the same horse, but only by the skin of his teeth. They were in the lead after the dressage, and Mark admits his attitude was totally different. 'I know I was full of confidence, because I thought, look out folks, we won it last year, we're going well this year, and we're going to do another good test' – which they did.

Then he almost blew his chances by doing what on his own admission was 'a very silly thing. I forgot to start my stopwatch at the beginning of the steeplechase, so I had to guess the speed, and I got it wrong.' He was eleven seconds over the time and collected 8.8 penalties. On Phase D Great Ovation did 'his usual workmanlike job – nothing spectacular'. But they did go clear, and theirs was the fifth fastest time recorded. However, Richard Meade on Derek Allhusen's Laurieston was quicker all round and finished the two days on a total of 106.00, while Mark had accumulated 106.6. It really could not have been closer.

They jumped on the final day in reverse order. Mark went clear, but knew Laurieston was a careful show jumper, and saw the title disappearing. Then the most extraordinary thing happened. Richard went very steadily to ensure a clear round – obviously aware that the margin was so tight he could not afford to have a single fence down. Mark was standing in the collecting ring next to friend and colleague Dick Stillwell. 'I was resigned to being second when Dick said, "You know, he's going to have time faults!" I said, "Don't be so daft," then looked at the clock and realized that the situation was indeed beginning to hot up. I just couldn't watch. He jumped a clear round, but then they announced he had 1.25 time faults, so I won. I felt really sorry for Richard, but in a funny sort of way I felt that justice had been done. But I could hardly believe that having being so stupid to start with, I'd been given the title back again.'

The following year Great Ovation was entered again, and there was tremendous speculation in the press about what would happen if Mark Phillips and the horse won for the third year running. Sheila Willcox had done the triple, but on two different horses. 'There were all sorts of stories about having to give us the trophy outright,' says Mark, 'but that was the kiss of death, wasn't it? He pulled up lame after the steeplechase course, so that was the end of that little pipedream.'

In 1973 it was not all disaster, as the same year Mark got his first ride on the Queen's horse Columbus. In spite of two falls, at Luckington Lane and at the Lake, Mark returned to the stables saying he had just had the ride of his life. 'Compared to Great Ovation,' he says, 'the horse was a Rolls-Royce.' Within six weeks of that Badminton, Buckingham Palace announced that Her Royal Highness The Princess Anne and Lieut. Mark Phillips were engaged. They were married in November, and the following year's Badminton was very much a family affair for Mark and his new bride. Princess Anne finished fourth on the Queen's horse Goodwill, while the newly promoted Captain Phillips stormed home on Columbus, the first rider in the event's history to complete the three days with no jumping or time penalties and to win the championship on his dressage score of 40.33. Of that year he says, 'I genuinely believed at the time that I was riding the best horse in the world. I held all the aces. He never made a semblance of a mistake, and I could almost lay money that you couldn't find a picture of him in 1974 without his ears pricked, making a super job of every fence. It was just so easy for him. We'd got our act together in a big way, and it does help when you're riding the best horse.'

At the presentation Her Majesty could not have been more delighted, handing the trophy to her son-in-law for winning on her own horse. Mark recalls, 'It was a magic moment, and I was tempted to hand it back to her – after all, she was the owner.'

That whole period was a marvellous time for Mark Phillips, but as so often happens, the fat years were followed by the lean. His win in 1981 on Lincoln was therefore especially gratifying. In fact he rates it as 'the second real high point of my career at Badminton. I got almost as much satisfaction out of that win as I did from the first. I was lucky to win the second time, and the third time felt that because I was on the best horse if I did everything right he ought to have won. But with Lincoln I didn't have the same confidence. I'd been in the wilderness for quite a few years, and hadn't had a top horse. So it was really good to come back ten years after the first win, and in a funny sort of way I felt as though I'd arrived again, and it's always nice to come back after everyone has written you off.'

Being 'written off' is perhaps putting it a bit strongly, though it is true that Mark went through a period of scant success. More recently he has built up a stock of promising young horses, and now runs his own, highly successful annual championships in the grounds of his home at Gatcombe Park. And it is that side of his career, as a trainer and course builder, that many people see as having a direct influence on the future of Badminton itself. For it is Mark Phillips' name that is mentioned more than any other as a possible successor to the present Badminton director, Frank Weldon. That decision, like the annual outcome of the championships, is very much an unknown quantity. But Mark Phillips is certainly out of the same mould as Weldon, and as the director knows only too well, once you've got a winning formula – stick with it.

Sticking with the winning formula would certainly seem to be the motto of Lucinda Green, one of Britain's most remarkable horsewomen and the most successful rider ever to compete at Badminton, winning a staggering six times. But as her record-breaking wins have all been made on different horses she would be the first to tell you that every year was different, as the individual characters and abilities of her horses have made quite separate demands on her skills.

Rather surprisingly, Lucinda says it definitely does not make life easy going back as a multiple winner. The burden of success is not one that weighs heavily on her shoulders. 'I just don't think about it any more,' she says. 'You can't be vain. You just have to think, "Oh hell, let's get on with it, and do the best we can". It's that attitude that keeps me enjoying Badminton, otherwise it would just be one hard sweat trying to win and win again, and I just couldn't cope with that.'

Something else Lucinda admits to not being able to cope with is disappointment, which is why Badminton did not become a major ambition until the year before her first competition in 1972. 'At the beginning it was something so far out of my grasp, and since I was very young I've never got passionate about things I thought might be beyond me, in case I failed, and then wouldn't be able to handle the disappointment. Where Badminton was concerned I just loved eventing. I loved the challenge of teaching a horse, learning confidence with it, and going on to face more and more difficult fences. So each year we just went on to see how far we could get, from novice, to intermediate, then advanced, until one day you start thinking, maybe we *are* capable of doing Badminton.'

The competition in 1972 came as a 'logical conclusion' after being in the winning team of the Junior European Championships at Punchestown the previous autumn. Experiencing a mixture of elation at having qualified for the competition and awe at her surroundings, Lucinda remembers nothing of her first walk around the course. 'It was an abyss of total dispair,' but, she says, 'I remember vividly my second walk, on which Mark Phillips kindly escorted me. I was very wound up, and expected to be told inch for inch where to put every foot and how to jump each fence. But Mark never really said anything. Every time we got to a fence he just said "kick on", regardless of the shape or combination. "Just kick on" the whole way round. Then at the end of the walk I had one of the worst nose bleeds I ever had in my life, because the pressure of the whole thing was beginning to build up in me. But when I came to ride the course all I remembered, in the back of my mind, were those two words, and it was the best advice that anybody could have given to a scared little number of eighteen trying to get round her first Badminton.' She had one stop on the course, at Tom Smith's Walls. 'I came in too fast, being a bit inexperienced about the whole thing, and I'll never forget pulling on the right rein to jump the second part on the walls, and feeling the rein just slip away through my fingers. It was a very hard lesson to learn, never to wear leather gloves on cross-country, because they get wet with the horse's sweat, and the reins just go straight through your hands.' That apart, it was a happy first Badminton. She had drawn number 34, which together added up to seven – 'my lucky number'. A dressage score of 83 put them in contention after the first day, and in spite of the stop on the cross-country, Be Fair had one of the fastest times of the day, and with no show jumping penalties to add they finished fifth. For the young Miss Prior-Palmer it was a magical moment. 'I was barely out of juniors, but there I was, in the top five at Badminton, up with the names of riders I'd hero-worshipped for years. It was the most extraordinary feeling.'

For the next twelve months the pair were on the crest of a wave. They were short-listed for the Olympics, and went back to Badminton 'knowing what to expect, rather than making a journey into darkness, the way we had the year before'. They were second after the dressage, but on cross-country day had a ride that Lucinda still describes as 'the roughest, most unenjoyable ride of my life'. The first hiccup came at the third fence, the Coffin. Be Fair fought for his head all the way into the first element, and Lucinda admits that she was not experienced enough to know how to cope with him. 'I kept a hold saying "slow, slow, slow", and as he came up to the rails, he didn't even realize they were there, and almost stopped, leaned over them, and to his eternal credit took off, and got just half his body over. We scrambled the rest of the way, down into the bog at the bottom of the ditch, then up the bank on the other side and over the second set of rails. We were all wrong, and made a total mess of it. But once we were over I remember hearing all the spectators scream and shout, and that put us right back on course.' There were no more hairy moments with the horse; from then on it was the course that was the source of grief. 'It had so many drops,' she recalls, 'they came one after the other, and a couple of them really hurt on landing.' They went clear, but Lucinda admits, on getting back to the stable, that she thought 'If this is what Badminton is about then it's not for me'.

Of the sixty-nine runners only thirty, less than half, survived to jump on the third day. Discovering that many of the other riders felt the same way about the course as she did helped Lucinda to overcome her disappointment, and made her realize just how fine is the line that exists between getting the course right and making a mistake. That year, the balance was tipped just enough to make the course downright uncomfortable. But in spite of her discomfort, Lucinda and Be Fair were way out in front, a clear 22 points ahead of Richard Meade on Eagle Rock. It gave her two fences in hand, but she knew she could so easily lose them on the final obstacle in the show jumping, a treble. She admits, 'I've never had much of an eye for a stride, and I remember coming round the corner, seeing the treble and thinking, "Oh my God, I'm going to have all three down, and that will be that". So I just sat there, and Be Fair got it absolutely right.' As they landed, she experienced for the first time the incredible roar of public acclaim that rolls across the arena from the stands to engulf the winner in the first few seconds of championship. To Lucinda, it was 'real tingle stuff – an echo of what I felt inside. And when I was presented with the trophy and they played the National Anthem, that was extraordinary. I'd had a great feeling of patriotism when we won the European Championships, but then I was part of a team. This was the first time it had ever happened to me individually. It was just Be Fair and me. We'd known each other since I was fifteen, we'd "gone to school together". I had such pride in my horse, it was just a fairy tale. I later drove the horse home myself because I wanted to be on my own with Be Fair, and as I motored out of Badminton I heard on the radio news that "Lucinda Prior-Palmer and Be Fair have won the Badminton championships". It was an extraordinary feeling. Whenever anyone says, "What was your greatest moment?" they all expect me to say the World Championships in 1982. And yes, that was important, but nothing could ever surpass that first win at Badminton. As far as I was concerned, it was a competition that other people won – better, more experienced riders than me. But suddenly I had won, and that feeling of initial excitement and joy has always been there.'

If 1973 was the year when Lucinda learnt how sweet it is to win, 1974 was the year when she experienced the sour taste of defeat. They naturally started the competition as favourites to win, but the three days began badly in the dressage arena, when a television camera between two judging boxes so distracted Be Fair that he just backed off during the counter canter movement, and would not go near the end of the arena. Her mark of 53.33 was not disastrous – it put her in the top ten, but not as highly placed as she would have liked. To compensate, she says she 'made the stupidest vow I've ever made in my life – I decided that we would take the most difficult route through each fence, regardless, just to pay the horse back for doing the dirty on me in the dressage.' The result was catastrophic. In spite of being warned about the bad going at the Crooked S, she still took the middle route, and slid into the first element to cartwheel over the fence in one of the most spectacular falls ever seen at Badminton. Both horse and rider were badly winded,

Lucinda Green on Beagle Bay 1984.
Right: Lucinda Green on Beagle Bay in the cross country, 1982.

but they continued. Lucinda reasoned that 'if I pulled out we would both sit there and think about it, and probably lose our nerve and never go again'. The horse went clear on show jumping day, and they finished 29th. Three days later, Be Fair couldn't move. The deep bruising had finally taken its toll, and Lucinda was disgusted with herself. Her father put the whole episode into perspective by reminding her, 'You're out there to get round the course clear, not to show off'. It was one of the hard lessons she learnt from Badminton, and came at the start of a whole run of disasters. But she is philosophical about the experience, saying, 'I'm convinced that anybody who's really going to get to the top, in whatever they do, has to go through a really bad, testing time. It's sort of God's way of finding out what you're made of.'

Whichever way you look at it, 1976 was the year Lucinda proved beyond all doubt that what she is made of is the stuff from which true champions are honed. After the dressage she and Wide Awake were in second place. Lucinda remembers walking the course on the day before the cross-country and hearing someone shout at her as she was sizing up the Luckington Lane fences, 'Going to win again this year then?' to which she replied, 'Don't be so silly – of course I'm not' – though she says, 'At the back of my mind I had this extraordinary feeling that we were. I'm always full of self doubt, but this time I felt it was going to be all right.'

She had been riding Wide Awake for almost four years and found that the Badminton atmosphere somehow worked wonders for him. 'We were really in harmony, and it was beautiful. On cross-country day he went like he'd never gone

before. It was majestic.' The horse went clear on day two, and again in the show jumping ring. She was a winner for the second time, and could not believe that the incredible moment of 1973 was being repeated.

Then, just as she was enjoying the heady euphoria of the moment, fate dealt the cruellest blow ever to hit a Badminton winner. Wide Awake dropped dead. This is how Lucinda described to me what happened. 'I shall never forget it. It's as if it was yesterday. We were standing at the side of the collecting ring, so the rest of the winners could come out before we made a little lap of honour on our own. As I was waiting, I saw a cherry picker [a mobile camera crane] go up behind one of the stands in front of me. As I was watching it, he reared up. He was a funny young horse anyhow, and did all sorts of crazy things, so it never struck me as anything unusual. But then he didn't stop, he kept on going up and down, and then he started to go sideways, and to run, though his back end didn't seem to come with him. I can't remember if I fell off, or got off, but I was on my feet, holding onto the reins, and he just went mad. Instinctively I knew he was going to die. It was just so wrong, the whole look of it. I think perhaps he'd broken his back – I really don't know, but it only took about fifty or sixty seconds. I'm actually glad that I was involved with it, part of what was happening, and not watching. It must have been horrible for the people who were watching, but because I was involved, somehow it wasn't so horrendous. Then suddenly, he went down, and that was that. Finished. Such a glorious moment, and then suddenly there was nothing. In a funny sort of way I knew it was all too good to be true, because it had been a blueprint of what had happened in 1973. We never knew what had caused it, perhaps it was a brain haemorrhage or a nerve arrest. But at least he knew nothing about it. It was very quick, and in a situation like that, you have to think that way.'

Undaunted, in 1977 she was back riding Killaire, owned by Mr. C. Cyzer of Horsham in Sussex, and Mrs H. Straker's horse George, who had managed to dump most of his previous riders and was offered to Lucinda just four weeks before the competition. 'It was very much hats over the windmill,' she says. 'Killaire was a wonderful old Irish hunter, safe as houses, who gave me a lovely ride. But George was another kettle of fish. That year we had a bounce into the lake on the fast route, with a single stride between the rails, and an overturned boat if you went the long way. I knew Killaire could manage it, but I was convinced George could never do it. He was renowned as a faller, but sitting in the box before I was due to ride his owner said, "Look Lucinda, that horse has hunted for years. I promise he'll go through the bounce". I thought, right, if he falls, it's not my fault, it's your fault. I was sick and weak with terror, and I'd got frozen on the roads and tracks. We'd had the most horrendous steeplechase ride, when he'd broken one of the ground rails because he'd ridden so badly. And I was thinking, if that's what he does with the steeplechase, he obviously didn't give a damn, so what's he going to do when he meets three foot eleven of Frank Weldon's timber?' What he did was to sail through without touching a thing. He even made the bounce, faultlessly, through the lake, leaving Lucinda feeling 'very guilty that I had ever doubted him'.

Killaire had a fence down in the show jumping, and George had 0.25 of a time penalty against him. But neither penalty was enough to rob them of their overnight positions. Killaire finished third, and George won. So it was third time lucky in 1977, and more than anyone could hope for to win again. But she did. In 1979 Killaire had *his* moment of glory. He took the lead in the dressage, and stayed there

Above: Richard Walker on Pasha, winners in 1969.
Right: Mark Todd and Southern Comfort, winners in 1980.

*Mark Todd on Charisma, second in 1984 before
going on to Olympic success at Los Angeles.*

for all three days. 'It was bliss,' is how Lucinda recalls that victory, on a horse for which she feels special affection. 'That lovely, lovely horse was never cut out to be an event horse. But he was so special, he was a great character.'

The 1977 win meant that Lucinda had set a new record – four wins. She remembers seeing a photograph of herself jumping into the water that year, and in the accompanying story the writer had speculated that if she could win Badminton four times, there was no reason why she should not go on winning. It was a nice thought, but Lucinda began to have her doubts. She then went through a 'dry' period in competition, not just at Badminton, but generally. Remembering that time, she says, 'I knew I'd had my moment. I was the girl of the seventies and I was never going to be anything else. It was a terrible feeling really. I knew I'd had more luck than fifteen people put together, and that it had just come to an end. It was rather a sad feeling, really. But then at the end of 1980 David came along [her husband David Green] and it all became fun again – and then suddenly the success came back.' She won Badminton for the fifth time in 1983 on Regal Realm, and again the following year on Beagle Bay. Both horses were owned by her sponsors, SR Direct Mail, whose backing will enable her to continue riding competitively for several years to come. But Lucinda no longer thinks about winning, and says, 'I must never expect to win it again, because I might never even get near, and then you start thinking, "Oh, I must do it again", and that would ruin it, it wouldn't be fun any more. It would become something you *had* to do, rather than one of those incredible things that just might happen.' But there is one thing that keeps niggling at the back of Lucinda's mind. Seven is her lucky number, so maybe the fates *do* still have one more of those 'incredible moments' lined up for her.

Considering the reputation that Badminton has as a world class event, it is perhaps surprising that so few foreign riders have claimed the championship. There have been only six. Two of them have been Irish riders: Captain M. A. Darley, who won in 1952 on Emily Little, and Major Eddie Bolan, thirteen years later, riding Durlas Eile. In 1951, the first year that the competition was 'open to the world', it was won by the Swiss cavalry Captain H. Schwarzenbach on Vae Victis, while 1960 and 1961 belonged to the Australians. In 1960 they wiped the board at Badminton. Bill Roycroft won on Our Solo, with Laurie Morgan second, less than four points behind, on Salad Days, and two more Australian riders, N. Lavis and J. Kelly, in fourth and tenth places respectively, on Mirrabooka and Adlai. Later that year the Australian team went on to win the team gold medal at the Rome Olympics, and in 1961 Laurie Morgan returned to Badminton with Salad Days to take the Whitbread Trophy. Then, for fourteen years from the late 1960s and throughout the 1970s, the Whitbread Trophy stayed in British hands. It took a New Zealander, Mark Todd, to break the mould in 1980.

As a young Pony Club rider, living on the other side of the world, Mark Todd's was a most unlikely introduction to Badminton. 'I read about it,' he says, 'in a story about a girl who had this horse that nobody else could ride. She tamed him and took him to Badminton – and that was the first time I'd ever heard of it.' It sounds like the start of a Mills and Boon saga, but the fictional 'storybook Badminton' soon became reality as Mark Todd saw photographs of the competition in the Australian equestrian press. His imagination was fired by 'wonderful photographs of horses and riders flying through the air over fences that looked unjumpable, and that made it a real challenge'. The logistics of actually getting to Badminton and even to the Olympic Games, which became his burning ambition, did not mean a lot to a twelve-year-old. Suffice it to say that the ambition became a reality, and after years of dogged determination he found himself competing at international level, with the chance of coming to England. He first set eyes on Badminton in 1979 as a spectator, and after years of anticipation found it looked 'big – but not impossible. I think I'd built it up so much in my imagination that when I saw it, I wasn't totally horrified by it'. A year later, with a horse called Southern Comfort, which he had found on a New Zealand farm, he qualified to compete at Badminton. After the dressage phase he was within 20 points of the leader and decided, 'I've got nothing to lose, so we'll have a real cut at it,' adding, 'ignorance is bliss'. (Haven't we heard that before!) It was one of the most difficult courses for years, and hardly anyone went round clear inside the time.' He managed both, and obviously the gods were with him, as there were several moments that could have ended in disaster. At the Sunken Road, Diana 'Tiny' Clapham was in front of him, and clearly having difficulty with her horse Windjammer. Mark saw her disappear off to the left, and thought she was getting out of his way, but just as he got within two strides of the fence he saw her approaching for the second time, and the two riders went over almost simultaneously.

A little further on, at the Footbridge, Southern Comfort drifted off to the right, heading for the ditch on the landing site. Mark threw his weight to the back of the saddle, and although the horse landed on his knees and skidded along the ground, they somehow managed to stay together and keep going. Then, coming into the Lake, he could see 'Two men in bowler hats standing in the middle of the run shaking hands and talking to each other. I screamed at them to get out of the way, and they both started to run, banged into each other and ended up standing still, so I just rode round them.' Mark Todd and Southern Comfort finished the day inside the time and in third place. Mark was delighted. 'Just to be at Badminton was amazing,' he says. 'There I was among all the top event riders in the world, and just being part of it was very special – but to finish the second day in third place was more than I could have ever hoped for.'

Then, on show jumping day, the impossible happened. Mark and Southern Comfort went clear. He was waiting to collect his third place rosette when Lucinda Green, who was lying second, had a foot in the water, and Mark moved up a place. Last to go was Helen Butler, in the lead on Merganzer with two fences in hand. The roar of the crowd told him she had four fences down, and suddenly Mark, the almost unknown rider from New Zealand, was the Badminton champion. After the presentation he went straight to the press tent to ring home. It was three o'clock in the morning when his parents picked up the telephone to hear their son yelling down the line, 'Guess what! I've won.' 'Don't be silly,' was the reply – but he had, and it was only the first step in realizing what had been a boyhood goal. As he says, 'Winning Badminton proved that I could compete successfully at top level, and that made all the difference to me.' In 1984 he came second on Charisma before going on to win the individual gold medal at the Los Angeles Olympics. He almost won the Whitbread championships again in 1985 on his Olympic horse, but after taking the lead on day two he dropped a pole in the show jumping ring, and the trophy passed instead to Virginia Holgate. Anyone who can travel from the other side of the world to realize a lifelong ambition isn't likely to give up trying for that second win just yet. As Mark Todd says, 'No matter how many times I ride at Badminton, it will always be a challenge, and while I don't ever expect to win as many times as Lucinda, twice would be nice.'

Meanwhile there must be event riders in every major equestrian nation in the world thinking how nice it would be to win just once. No American, for instance, has ever taken the title, in spite of strong contention from top riders such as former world champion Bruce Davidson and Olympic horsewoman Torrance Watkins Fleischmann. In spite of Europe's fine equestrian traditions, and regular attempts by top Dutch, Austrian, German, French and Swedish riders over the past thirty years, the title has crossed the Channel only once.

There is no doubt that Badminton, like the competitors who gather to meet its annual challenge, is special. It's the classic three day event. As so many riders have said, 'It's the one competition we all want to win,' so while riders and horses are prepared to go on offering their skill and courage for the ultimate test, let us hope that Badminton will always be there to meet the challenge with a course and competition that remain, quite simply, the biggest and best in the world.

Past Winners at Badminton

1949	..	Mr J. Shedden on Mrs Home Kidston's Golden Willow
1950	..	Capt J. A. Collings on Miss G. H. Crystal's Remus
1951	..	Capt H. Schwarzenbach (Switzerland) on Vae Victis
1952	..	Capt M. A. Q. Darley on Emily Little
1953	..	Major L. Rook on Mrs J. R. Baker's Starlight
1954	..	Miss M. Hough on Bambi
1955	..	*(Windsor)* Major F. W. C. Weldon on Kilbarry
1956	..	Lt-Col F. W. C. Weldon on Kilbarry
1957	..	Miss S. M. Willcox on High and Mighty
1958	..	Miss S. M. Willcox on High and Mighty
1959	..	Mrs J. Waddington on Airs and Graces
1960	..	*(Great Badminton)* Mr W. Roycroft (Australia) on Our Solo *(Little Badminton)* Capt M. F. Whiteley on Peggoty
1961	..	*(Great Badminton)* Mr L. R. Morgan (Australia) on Salad Days *(Little Badminton)* Capt J. P. E. Welch on Mr Wilson
1962	..	*(Great Badminton)* Miss A. Drummond-Hay on Merely-a-Monarch *(Little Badminton)* Mrs P. M. Crofts on Mr H. Graham-Clark's Priam
1964	..	*(Great Badminton)* Capt J. R. Templer on M'Lord Connolly *(Little Badminton)* Mrs J. Waddington on Glenamoy
1965	..	*(Great Badminton)* Major E. A. Boylan (Ireland) on Durlas Eile *(Little Badminton)* Capt M. F. Whiteley on The Poacher
1967	..	Miss C. Ross-Taylor on Jonathan
1968	..	Miss J. Bullen on Our Nobby
1969	..	Mr Richard Walker on Pasha
1970	..	Mr Richard Meade on the Combined Training Committee's The Poacher
1971	..	Lt M. A. P. Phillips on his own and Miss F. Phillips' Great Ovation
1972	..	Lt M. A. P. Phillips on his own and Miss F. Phillips' Great Ovation
1973	..	Miss L. Prior-Palmer on Be Fair
1974	..	Capt M. A. P. Phillips on H. M. The Queen's Columbus
1976	..	Miss L. Prior-Palmer on Mrs V. Phillips' Wide Awake
1977	..	Miss L. Prior-Palmer on Mrs H. C. Straker's George
1978	..	Mrs T. Holderness-Roddam on Mrs S. Howard and Mrs T. Holderness-Roddam's Warrior
1979	..	Miss L. Prior-Palmer on Mr C. Czyer's Killaire
1980	..	Mr M. J. Todd (New Zealand) on Southern Comfort III
1981	..	Capt M. A. P. Phillips on Range Rover Team's Lincoln
1982	..	Mr R. J. H. Meade on George Wimpey Plc's Speculator III
1983	..	Mrs L. Green on SR Direct Mail Ltd.'s Regal Realm
1984	..	Mrs L. Green on SR Direct Mail Ltd.'s Beagle Bay
1985	..	Miss V. Holgate on British National Life Assurance's Priceless
1986	..	Mr Ian Stark on Sir Wattie

DRESSAGE

The object of dressage is the harmonious development of the physique and ability of the horse. As a result, it makes the horse calm, supple and keen, thus achieving perfect understanding with its rider.

Marking

Each of the 20 movements in the test and of the 4 sets of collective marks is awarded from 0 to 10 good marks by each of the three judges. There are therefore 240 good marks which can be awarded by each judge.

Any penalties incurred for errors of course are deducted from each judge's sheet and the total marks of the three judges are then averaged. The good marks thus obtained are subtracted from 240 to express the score in penalty points. A factor of .6 is then applied in addition to the selected Multiplying Factor.

Errors of Course

The test must be executed from memory. Errors of course or wrong sequence of movements, whether corrected or not, are penalized as follows:

First error	. . .	2 marks
Second error	. . .	4 marks
Third error	. . .	8 marks
Fourth error	. . .	Elimination

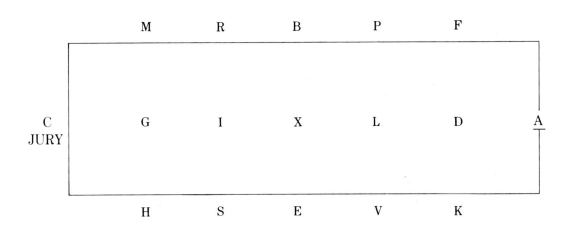

On a full size dressage arena there are seventeen markers denoted by letters of the alphabet (see diagram above). All movements in the test must be performed at the markers as indicated on the left hand side of the test sheet opposite.

FEI Three-day Event Dressage Test (1975)

		TEST	MAX MARKS
1	A	Enter at a working canter	10
	X	Halt – Immobility – Salute – Proceed at working trot	
2	C	Track to the left	
	S	Medium trot	10
	EBE	Circle to the left 20 metres diameter	
	EV	Medium trot	
3	V	Working trot	
	A	Down centre line	10
	L	Circle to the left 10 metres diameter	
4	LS	Half-pass (left)	10
5	C	Halt – Rein back 5 steps – Proceed at working trot without halting	10
6	R	Medium trot	
	BEB	Circle to the right 20 metres diameter	10
	BP	Medium trot	
7	P	Working trot	
	A	Down centre line	10
	L	Circle to the right 10 metres diameter	
8	LR	Half-pass (right)	10
9	C	Halt – Immobility 5 seconds – Proceed at working trot	10
10	HXF	Change rein at extended trot (rising)	10
	F	Working trot	
11	KXM	Change rein at extended trot	10
	M	Working trot	
12	C	Medium walk	
	HSXPF	Extended walk	10
	F	Medium walk	
13	A	Working canter – Circle to the right 10 metres diameter	10
14	AC	Serpentine 3 loops, the first and the third true canter, the second counter-canter	10
15	MXK	Change rein at extended canter	10
	K	Working trot	
16	A	Working canter – Circle to the left 10 metres diameter	10
17	AC	Serpentine 3 loops, the first and the third true canter, the second counter-canter	10
18	HXF	Change rein at extended canter	10
	F	Working trot	
19	A	Down centre line	10
	L	Working canter to the right	
20	G	Halt – Immobility – Salute	10
		Leave arena at walk on a long rein TOTAL	200

Collective marks:
1. Paces (freedom and regularity)   10
2. Impulsion (desire to move forward, elasticity of the steps and engagement of the hind quarters)   10
3. Submission (attention and obedience, lightness and freedom of the movements, acceptance of the bit)   10
4. Position, seat of the rider, correct use of the aids   10

240

To be deducted:
Errors of the course and omissions are penalized:

1st time	2 marks	3rd time	8 marks
2nd time	4 marks	4th time	Elimination

Note The working, medium and extended trots must be executed 'sitting' unless the term 'rising' is used in the text.

SPEED
AND ENDURANCE

This test is to prove the speed, endurance and jumping ability of the true cross-country horse when he is well trained and brought to the peak of condition. At the same time it demonstrates the rider's knowledge of pace and use of his horse across country.

The test consists of four distinct and independent phases, which follow one another and are performed at a stretch, with only one halt of 10 minutes to allow for a veterinary inspection.

It is scored entirely on a penalty basis. The Optimum Time for each phase is calculated on the distances and speeds shown in the Summary. Completing any phase within the Optimum Time incurs 0 penalty, but exceeding the Optimum Time is penalized according to the scale of penalties below. In addition, faults at the obstacles are penalized according to the appropriate table.

Summary of Phases

Phase	Nature	Distance	Speed	Optimum Time	Time Limit
		Metres	Metres per min.	Mins. Secs.	Mins. Secs.
A	Roads & Tracks	4400	220	20.00	24.00
B	Steeplechase	3105	690	4.50	9.00
C	Roads & Tracks	9900	220	45.00	54.00
	Vet. Inspection	—	—	10.00	—
D	Cross-Country	6952	570	12.12	30.54

Time Penalties

Phases A and C.   A Competitor is penalized 1 penalty point for each second in excess of the Optimum Time up to the Time Limit which is ⅕th more than the Optimum Time. Exceeding the Time Limit incurs elimination.

Phase B.   A Competitor is penalized .8 of a penalty point for each second in excess of the Optimum Time up to the Time Limit which is twice the Optimum Time. Exceeding the Time Limit incurs elimination.

Phase D.   A Competitor is penalized .4 of a penalty point for each second in excess of the Optimum Time up to the Time Limit which is based on a speed of 225 metres per minute. Exceeding the Time Limit incurs elimination.

Examination of Horses (between Phases C and D)

There will be a break of 10 minutes in the timetable for each horse. During this interval a committee composed of a veterinary surgeon and two judges will examine each horse in order to decide whether it is fit to continue. Should they decide any horse is unfit, they are responsible for ordering its immediate withdrawal.

Faults at Obstacles

Faults at obstacles are penalized, according to the following table, only if they occur within an area surrounding each obstacle, known as the Penalty Zone.

First refusal, run-out, circle of horse at obstacle	20 penalties
Second refusal, run-out, circle of horse at same obstacle	40 penalties
Third refusal, run-out, circle of horse at same obstacle	Elimination
Leaving penalty zone before jumping the obstacle	20 penalties
Fall of horse and/or rider at obstacle	60 penalties
Second fall of horse and/or rider at obstacle during the steeplechase phase	Elimination
Third fall of horse and/or rider at obstacle during the Cross-Country phase	Elimination
Omission of obstacle or red or white flag	Elimination
Retaking an obstacle already jumped	Elimination
Jumping obstacle in wrong order	Elimination

The penalties are cumulative

Assistance

Forbidden Assistance: Outside assistance is forbidden, under penalty of elimination. Any intervention by a third party, whether solicited or not, with the object of facilitating the task of the rider or of helping his horse is considered illegal assistance.

Exception: After a fall or if a competitor dismounts, he may be assisted to catch his horse, to adjust his saddlery, to remount or to be handed any part of his equipment while he is dismounted or after he has remounted. Whips, headgear or spectacles may be handed to a competitor without dismounting.

JUMPING

The test on the third day is not an ordinary showjumping competition, nor a test of style or endurance. Its sole object is to prove that, on the day after a severe test of endurance, horses have retained the suppleness, energy and obedience necessary for them to continue in service.

The test is over a course of between 700 and 800 metres with 10 to 12 obstacles, to be carried out at a speed of 400 metres per minute.

Time
Completing the course in less than the time is not rewarded but a competitor exceeding the time is penalized at a rate of a quarter of a mark for every second in excess of the time up to the Time Limit, after which he is eliminated.

Faults at Obstacles

Knocking down an obstacle or foot in water	5 penalties
First disobedience	10 penalties
Second disobedience in the whole test	20 penalties
Third disobedience in the whole test	Elimination
Jumping an obstacle in the wrong order	Elimination
Error of course not rectified	Elimination
Fall of horse or rider	30 penalties

General Conditions

Rules
The Competition is governed by the FEI Rules for Three Day Events (1983).

Disclaimer of Liability
Save for death or personal injury caused by the negligence of the organizers or anyone for whom they are in law responsible, neither the Badminton Horse Trials Committee, The British Horse Society nor the British Equestrian Federation, nor any agent, employee or representative of these bodies accepts any liability for any accident, loss, damage, injury or illness to horses, owners, riders, spectators, land or any other person or property whatsoever, whether caused by their negligence, breach of contract or in any other way whatsoever.

Metric Conversion Table

Fences

Metres	Feet
0.3	1
0.6	2
0.675	2' 3"
0.75	2' 6"
0.9	3
0.975	3' 3"
0.99	3' 4"
1.05	3' 6"
1.098	3' 8"
1.125	3' 9"
1.2	4
1.35	4' 6"
1.5	5
1.77	5' 11"
1.8	6
2.1	7
2.4	8
2.7	9
2.76	9' 2"
3.3	11
3.6	12
3.9	13
10.8	36

Speed and Endurance

Metres	Yards
100	109.9
200	219.8
220	241.8
225	247.3
300	329.7
400	439.6
500	549.5
570	626.4
600	659.3
690	758.2
700	769.2
800	879.1
1000	1099.0
3105	3412.0 (1.94 miles)
4400	4835.2 (2.75 miles)
6952	7639.6 (4.34 miles)
9900	10879.1 (6.18 miles)

Footnote

In the summer of 1986 Frank Weldon built six extra fences within the confines of Badminton Park which had no connection whatsoever with the Whitbread Championships. There was a coffin, a flight of three steps, a large ditch and rail, and fences offering combinations and bounces. Their purpose? To provide a training ground for British riders and their horses before tackling the competition at Bialy Bor in Poland in September.

Since 1977 British teams preparing for major international championships used the excellent facilities of Wyle in Wiltshire with Lady Hugh Russell as host, mentor and cross-country trainer. But when the estate was sold out of the Russell family just after the 1986 World Championships at Gawler, the Duke of Beaufort offered Badminton as a new training arena. It means that from now on, whenever Britain sends a team to any European, World or Olympic three day event championship, horses and riders will be schooled and prepared in all three disciplines using a specially prepared course at Badminton – in essence, just as they did in 1949, 1952 and 1956.

The vision that prompted 'Master' to offer Badminton for that very first competition has finally come full circle.

INDEX

Note: Horses names are in *italics*
     numerals in *italics* indicate photographs

Adlai, 176
Airs and Graces, 32, 167
Allhusen, Major Derek, 47, 170
Amateur Athletics Association, 96
Anne, Princess, 32, 63, 92, 141, 144, 162-4
Any Chance, 109
Armada dishes, 90, 160, 162
Autumn Venture, 108
Avon and Bristol Federation of Boy's Clubs, 92,
     132

Badminton, Ball, 138; Bond Street, 69, 90, 100;
     Bus, 76; Committee 61, 72, 88; Horse Trials,
     56, 62, 64, 66, 72; Roll of Honour, 160; Winners
     List, 158, 181
Ball, Alan, 132
Bale, Peter, 75, 76, 79, 80
Bambi, 26, 58, 59
Bambi V, 24, 27, 79, 167
Banbridge Boy, 24, 26
Barberry, 168
BBC, 70, 74, 75, 76, 79, 80, 81, 82, 84, 96, 100, 107,
     115, 116, 122, 126, 127, 157
Beagle Bay, *174*, *175*, 178
Beaufort, Duke of (Master), 11, 14, 27, 28, *29*,
     30, 31, 32, 37, 41, 42, 54, 56, 62, *63*, 64, 65, 68,
     80, 84, 85, *86*, *99*, 120
Beaufort, Hunt, 15, 68, 95, 98;
     Hunt Pony Club, 60, 124, 169
Be Fair, 172-3, 174
Belascoe, Jack, 75, 76, 79, 80, 85
Biddlecombe, W. C., 19
Bishop, George, 116
Blaser, Captain A., 22
Bleak Hills, 34
Blue Book, 14, 95, 96
Bolan, Major Eddie, 179
Bolton, Brigadier L., 27
Borwick, Major Peter, 12
Bowden, Major Geoffrey, 95, 103
Bowden-Smith, Brigadier 'Bogey', 12
British Army (military), 28, 56, 57, 60, 87
British Cavalry (Weedon), 12, 21

British Horse Society (BHS), 12, 14, 15, 19, 28,
     58, 65, 66, 68, 70, 76, 129, 186
British Show Jumping Association (BSJA), 19,
     20, 32
Bromley-Gardner, Caroline, 96-7
Bromley-Gardner, Lt-Col. R., 97
Brookes, Jane, 87, 88, 90, 92, 106
Brookes, Jill, 68
Brookes-Ward, Raymond, 37, 51, 79, 82, 84, 85
Buccleauch, Duke of, 148
Buhler, Mr. Anton, 110
Bullen, Jane, 32, 47, 61, 113
Bullen, Jennie, 61
Butler, Helen, 180
Burgess, Pat, 149
Burghley Horse Trials, 28, 42, 148, 150, 162

Cameron-Hayes, John, 58
Castle, Major Ian, 105
Chapple, Charlie, 12, 38, *55*
Charisma, *118*, 180
Clapham, Diana 'Tiny', *94*, 106, 179
Clarke, Lorna, 142, 162
Collings, Captain Tony, 16, 20, *21*, 24, 26, 59
Colombus, *83*, 85, *161*, 170, 171
Combined Training Committee, 59, 60
Cornell, C., 12
Cornisham V, 168
Cotswold Equitation School, 16
Count de Bolebec, *99*, 114, 124
Countryman, 60
Cowgill, Brian, 81
Cox-Cox, Colonel Gordon, 28, 40, *41*, 42, 66, 75,
     76
Crispin, 24, 26, 60
Cubitt, Col. The Hon. C. 'Guy', 12, *17*
Czyer, Mr. C., 176

Daily Telegraph, 22, 70, 98
Dallas, Major Ronnie, 54, 88, 98, 113
Dandy, 27
Dandy Dick, 16
Darely, Captain M. A., 27, 179
Davidson, Bruce, 113, 116, *117*, 120, 126, 180
Davis, Claire, 149

Doublet, 32, 162
Drummond-Hay, Anneli, 32, 61, 169
Drummond-Hay, Jane, 24
Durlas Eile, 179
Dylan II, 134, 138, 141
Dyson, Major Derek, 53, 68, 69, 70, 76, 87, 88, 89, 100, *104*
Eagle Rock, 173
Ebony Green, 113
Edgar, Ted, 19
Edinburgh Woollen Mill, The, 148
Eilberg, Ferdi, 149
Electron, 141
Elizabeth II, 27, 32, 41, 60, 63, 85, 92, 162, 171
Emily Little, 27, 179
European Championships, 27, 28, 32, 42, 47, 58, 59, 61, 65, 74, 79, 148, 162, 168, 173

Fédération Equestre Internationale, (FEI), 12, 18, 30, 40, 54, 61, 186
Fermoy, 61
Fleischmann, Torrance Watkins, 111, 120, 180
Flemming, Barbara Slane, 149, 154
Fonblanque, Captain D. de, 12
Franks, Cliff, 126

Gardiner, Neil, 61
Gatcombe Park, 171
George, *33*, 176
Gillmore, Jim, 84, 91, 97, 98
Gisborne Park, 22
Glenburnie, 120, 148, 149, 150-3
Golden Willow, 16, *17*, 18-9, 20, 38
Gold Pot, 24
Goodwill, 162, *163*, 170
Grand Prix, 12, 16, 30
Gravière, Vicomte Jurien de la, 110, 113
Great Ovation, 169, 170
Green, David, *75*, *118*, 126, 132, *137*, *138*, 154, 178
Green, Lucinda, 32, *33*, 34, 42, 50, 64, *71*, 74, 85, *99*, 114, 116, *121*, 124, 132, 137, 154, 160, 171-79, *174*, *175*, 180
Greylag, 27
Guardian, 98
Gundry, Jane, 53, 68, *86*, 87, 88, 96, 101, 113
Gunners Gold Cup, 58
Gupwell, Brian, 54, *89*, 109
Gurdon, Madeleine, 126

Happy Knight, 22
Hall, Robert, 60
Harewood House, Yorkshire, 28, 61
Harland, Nick, 113

Harrington, Frank, 126
Heavy Weather, 58
High and Mighty, 32, 38, 60, *165*
Hill, Bertie, 24-5, 26, 27, 32, 58, 60, 162
Hill, Janet, 115, *125*
Hindley, Reg, 21, 22, 24, 26, *26*, 27, 58
Hingham, Brian, 98, 108, 113
Holderness-Roddam, Jane, *see* Bullen, Jane
Holgate, Virginia, *see* Leng, Virginia
Home Kidson, Mrs. 19
Horn, Col. Trevor, 12, 14, 15, 18, 37
Horse and Hound, 88, 91, 92
Horse of the Year Show, 79
Horse Trials Support Group, 49
Hough, Margaret, 24, 59, 79, 167
Hunt, Rachel, *77*, 134, 157, 158

Ingall, Sue, 68, 91, 101, 114

James, Dick, 108
J. J. Babou, 113
Jones, Sgt. Ben, 47
Jones, Vincent, 34
Junior European Championships, 164, 172

Kelly, J., 179
Kilbarry, 27, *31*, 38, *40*, *57*, 58, *59*, 59, 60, 61, 79, 168
Killaire, *33*, 176
Kingpin, 20
King's Troop, 57, 60, 76

Laurieston, 170
Lavis, N., 179
Lemieux, Robert, 116, 154
Leng, Virginia, 32, 64, *67*, 74, 84, 85, *111*, 116, *119*, 124, 125, 126, 128, 180
Lincoln, 171
Liza Mandy, 27, 58
Luczycwyhowska, Susan, 148
Luter, Michael and Janet, 100-1

Mahmud, 22
Mahon, Frank, 113, 141
Margaret, Princess, 27, 79, 84
Marsh, Ted, 60
Marshall, Mrs. N., 61
Mason, Claire, 116
Mason, Diana, 60
Massarella, Andrew, 19
Massarella, Ronnie, 19
Maxwell-Scott, Dame Jean, 148

McAulay, Jean, 149
McMeckin, Lady, 124
Meade, Richard, 32, 34, *37*, 47, 74, 160, *161*, *163*, 170, 173
Merely-a-Monarch, 32, 61, 169
Merganzer, 180
Michaelmas Day, 109
Midland Bank Championship, 49
Midnight Monarch II, 124
Miller, Sandi, 149
Miller, Sir John, 21, 24, *25*, 26, 162
Mirrabooka, 179
M'Lord Connolly, 42
Morgan, Laurie, 166, 179
Morgan, Lieutenant Christopher, 58
Moseley, Lt.-Col. R. 'Babe', 12, 40, *41*, 42
Mr. Panache, 125

National Light Horse Improvement Society, 90
Naylor-Leyland, Captain Michael, 24, 26
Newfield, 120
Nifikim, 113
Night Cap II, 116, 124, 125, 126, 128, 129, 153
Norland Nursery Training College, 122
Nyblaë, Colonel Gustav, 61

Oliver, Alan, 57
Oliver, Alison, 32, 162
Olympic Games, 11, 12, 22, 65, 74, 179; 1952, 16, 20, 24, 28, 42, 79; 1956, 42, 59, 60, 162; 1960, 169, 179; 1964, 42, 61; 1968, 47; 1984, 122, 146, 149, 180
Olympic Horse Trials, 22, 42
O'Neill, Tim, 70, 72, 73
Oram, Lieut. Cdr. John, 24, 26
Our Nobby, 32, 47
Our Solo, 179
Oxford Blue, 146, 148, 149

Parker, Katie, 114
Pasha, 168-9
Pegasus Club, 58
Petre, Joan, 88, 92, 106
Phillipa, 24, 26
Philip, Prince, 27
Phillips, Mark, 32, 34, 50, 51, 54, 61, *83*, 85, 160, *161*, 169-71
Philpot, Petrina, 125
Piglet II, *77*, 134
Pony Club Championships, 38
Porlock School of Equitation, 16, 24, 25, 26, 59
Priceless, 24, *67*
Princess Anne, *83*, *159*, 162, *163*
Prior-Palmer, Lucinda, *see* Green, Lucinda

Queen Mother, *29*, 79

Red Cross, 122, 132
Regal Realm, 178
Remus, 16, 20, *21*, 24, 26
Ritchie, Susan, 108
Rock On, 169
Rook, Major Laurence, 24, 26, 27, *31*, 32, 38, 40, 41, 58, 59, 60, 63, *63*, 88, 95, *104*, 113, 114, 162
Rooke, Lesley, 15
Rooke, Major Nelson, 15
Rosen, Count Clarence von, 12
Rothkirck, Count Leopold, 61
Royal Marines, 24; Band, 141
Roycroft, Bill, 179
Russell, Jim, 58
Russell, Lady Hugh, 149

Salad Days, 169, 179
Samuel Johnson, 61
Sandhurst, Royal Military College, 11
Sarah, Lady, 79
Savoyarde, 24, 26
Schwarzenbach, Hans, 24, 179
Schwerdt, Polly, 116, *130*, 134, 138
Sederholm, Lars, 52
Shannagh, *99*, 116, 132, 134
Shedden, John, 16, *17*, 18, 20, 38, 41
Sir Wattie, *35*, 116, 125, 134, 144, *146*, 148-58, *151*, *155*, *159*
Smythe, Pat, 19
Snowdon, Lord, 79
Snowshill Lad, 58
Somerset, David (Duke of Beaufort), 44, 56, 62, 63, 66, 68, 88, 97, 98, 110, 120
Southern Comfort, 179
Sparrow Hawk II, 116
Speculation, 24, 26, *26*, 27, 58
Speculator III, 160, *161*
sponsorship, 34, 61, 70, 72, 142, 148, 178
Springorum, Dr. B., 110
SR Direct Mail, 178
Stark, Jenny, 148, 149
Stark, Ian, *35*, 116, 120, 125, 134, 141, 142, *145*, *146*, 144-58, *151*, *155*, *159*
Starlight, 24, 26, 27, 38, 58, 59, 60, *XV*, *31*
Stealaway, 21, 22, 24, 26
Stella, 21, 24, *25*, 26, 27
Stibbe, Eddie, 108
Stillwell, Dick, 170
Stokes, W., 16
Stoneham, George, 53
Stowell Park, 58
Strachan, Clarissa, 154
Straker, Mrs. H., 176

Straker, Karen, 120
Strawson, Ginny, 116
Strike a Light, 100, 141
Sunday Telegraph, 62

Talbot-Ponsonby, Jack, 60
Tanzer, 120
Templar, Captain J., 42
The Artful Dodger, 116
The Poacher, 160, 168
Thornbury, Gilbert, 48, 52
Thomas, Hugh, 82, 84
Three-day event, 11, 12, 14, 19, 27, 32, 42, 44, 58, 74, 87;
    rules, 61; world, 120
Tidmarsh, Bernie, 109-10, 113
Todd, Mark, 53, 64, 109, *118,* 141, 148, 149, 156, *177, 178,* 178-80
Torloisk, 24
Trotter board, 123-4, 128
Trotter, Colonel W., 123
Tucker, Mike, 61, 82, 84, 126
Tudor Gal, 24, 26

Vae Victis, 22, 276
Viner, Fred, 84

Waddington, Sheila, *see* Willcox, Sheila
Waitjen, Herr Richard, 25
Walkabout, 132, II, *137*
Walker, Richard, 52, *166,* 168-9
Walter, Bill, 113
Wanklin, Joan, 73
Water Gypsy, 58
Weldon, Colonel Frank W. C., 27, *31,* 30-54, *40,* passim, 50-64, *57, 59, 62,* 65-73 passim, 79, 81, 82, 87, 88, 90, 95, 96, 97, 98, 103-142, *104,* passim, 150, 153, 160, 162, 169, 171
Wessex Yeomanry, 122, 123
Whitbread, Colonel Bill, 70, 72
Whitbread, 70, 72, 73, 116;
    Championships, 37, 56, 72, 73, 74, 87, 121, 179;
    Trophy, 32, 70, 72, 146, 180
Whiteley, Martin, 50
Wide Awake, 85, 173
Wierschkoff, Kitty, 111
Wild Venture 60
Williams, Dorian, 60, 76, 79, 84, 168
Willcox, Sheila, 32, 41, 42, 60, 64, 85, 160, 162-3, *165,* 168
Willis, Alan, 48, 52
Windjammer, 179
Winter Sun, 108
Woolridge, John and Lesley, 111-2

World Championships, 74, 148, 149, 172
Worshipful Company of Saddlers, 90
Wotherstone, Jonny, 74, 81, 82, 83

Young, Brian, 27
Young Pretender, 61

ACKNOWLEDGEMENTS

The publishers wish to thank the following copyright holders for their permission to reproduce the following: BBC Hulton Picture Library p. 8, 13, 14, 15, 19, 29 (top left and bottom left), 31, 59; Peter Harding p. 10, 17, 21, 25, 26, 29 (top right), 33, 36, 41, 43, 62, 138, 143, 161, 177; S&G Press Agency p. 17, 29, (bottom right), 40, 57, 165; Homer Sykes p. 55, 71, 99, 135. The remaining photographs are by Kit Houghton, and the drawings in Chapter 3 of the course jumps are by Caroline Bromley-Gardner. Picture research by Leslie Davy.